An Activist's Tale,

My Walk
With
Palestine

Fra Hughes

About the author

Fra Hughes & Pauline O'Hare, shortly after their engagement. Rome, Italy 2015

Fra Hughes is an independent, political activist living in Belfast, Ireland. He is the volunteer Director of Palestine Aid. By Politics, he is anti-imperialist, anti-colonialist, and anti-capitalist, he believes in a fairer world with social justice, a redistribution of wealth and an equality based society fit for all.

"The only thing necessary for the triumph of evil is for good men to do nothing." Edmund Burke

Published By: Green Cross Art & Bookshop Ltd

Dedicated to Pauline,
whose help and support made my Journey
with Palestine possible.

My walk with Palestine is not a political book even if the title makes it look like an activist story, which is true, it's the core of this sincere telling but it's above all a human story. The story of a man born and raised in a difficult city, Belfast, who self-acquired a sensibility towards injustice. It's a story about love, loving life and being positive towards it; loving the others especially those who are weak and need help, doing something even if it's teeny for them; love between a man and a woman who supports him and fears for his safety. He also loves her and misses her during his long difficult journey. This is an important aspect that I guess readers will capture as I did.

Another aspect is globalization and internet power that gave our teller access to a kind of information he was starving for, information that is much more pure than the one offered by mainstream media. Such information when received by a man like him changed his life by giving him a wider perspective of the world, a specific goal to achieve and a challenge to overcome.

Strong friendships that he tightened during his journey with some of the convoy participants and also ordinary people of the places where he spent few days or even a swift link he created with a young boy who followed the convoy while passing quickly are aspects of this telling that render it a human more than a political one.

This is the particularity of this telling, it's a real human story or even stories that Fra Hughes is generously sharing with the readers.

Sherif Salem
Egyptian Filmmaker

CONTENTS

ACKNOWLEDGEMENTS

INTRODUCTION

Part 1

Part 2

Part 3

Part 4

Part 5

ACKNOWLEDGMENTS

This book has been inspired by the resilience of the Palestinian people who have suffered invasion, colonisation, military occupation, siege and ethnic cleansing by the forces of Zionism, who are determined to erase Palestine from history.

From those suffering under occupation and siege, to those living in exile or in refugee camps, you have enlisted millions to support your call for justice and dignity for Palestine.

To my friends on the convoys, to those I met and those who helped me throughout my travels, I dedicate this book to you, the unsung heroes who support Palestine and give your time, energy, heart, commitment and sometimes your lives in the cause for freedom and nationhood for Palestine.

For Carole, Saeb, Paudy, John, Joe, Seamus, John Hurson, Harry, Richard, Uncle Yousef, Babagee, Mohammed Ali, Tony, Jeminah, Mark, Colin, Kevin Ovendun, Ron, George Galloway and every Palestinian in prison, in exile, in their graves and in refugee camps who never gave up - From the River to the Sea, Palestine will be free!

I want to thank Liam and Fiona Johnston who helped me bring the book to publication.

Introduction

This book has been written from memory and I apologise if I may have mixed up some of the dates, forgotten anyone who feels they should be included or missed out any relevant facts or events.

It is written as I remember it to have happened and I believe it to be a true and fair reflection of my actions, thoughts and deeds over 4 years between 2010 and 2014.

Fra Hughes
February 2018

PART 1

Background 1963 - 2009

Chapter 1

A bit about myself, I was born in Belfast, Ireland on October 21st 1963, the same year that John Fitzgerald Kennedy (JFK) President of the United States of America was assassinated in Dallas, Texas.

At the age of about four, my Mother Ursula Hughes née McSwiggan, noticed I was walking with a slight limp and after convincing my General Practitioner(GP) Dr. Michael McSorely that she was not an overprotective mother I was referred to the Royal Belfast Hospital for Sick Children where I was diagnosed by an Orthopaedic surgeon, Mr Piggott, as suffering from Perthes Disease, a malformation of the hip joint and avascular necrosis which is a painful condition that occurs when blood supply to the bone is disrupted. I spent several months in frog plaster and traction, as well as undergoing two separate operations to insert three metal screws and a metal plate into my left hip joint.

Untreated Perthes Disease leads to a shortening of the leg whereby one leg can be up to 12 inches shorter than the other. As you can imagine it was a very worrying time for my parents, a worry I was thankfully unaware of as I didn't really understand at that age what was happening. I trusted in a mother's love that everything would be ok.

It was a very successful operation and I have some fond memories of my six months at Musgrave Park Hospital, unable to walk, being given school lessons with several other hospitalised kids in a makeshift classroom and following my hospital release, further tutoring at home with Ms Rutledge. I remember the kindness of family, friends and neighbours towards me, as the young boy who sat outside his front door, on a blanket, unable to walk or run or play with the other kids in the street and who had to be carried everywhere. Treats, sweeties and money from those passing by along with a wee pat on the head were the order of the day. With a bed in the front room for convenience, this was to become my whole world.

I have grown up to be able to play football and squash, learn to swim, play golf, practice Shotokan Karate and jog six miles several times a week. I have twinges and pains infrequently but no major concerns thank goodness.

I attended Holy Family Catholic Primary School on the Limestone Road for boys aged between five and eleven. It was only a five minute walk from where I grew up, beside the Waterworks, a man-made reservoir for collecting drinking water for the people of Belfast. It also serves as a public park with two lakes and waterfalls. Like many kids I cried the first day mum left me at the gates of my new school. I guess the illness in my formative years had given us a strong bond, one I did not want to let go off lightly. Later having failed the eleven plus, (grammar school entrance exam) I went to St Patrick's Secondary School, Bearnageeha, for boys aged between eleven and eighteen. *(Bearnageeha in Irish translates as the windy gap)*. Situated on the Antrim Road, it was a school of hard knocks and a few hard men.

I remember in 1976 at aged 13, pupils stormed the gates and bypassed the teachers who stood valiantly trying to prevent our exit, a mass walk out. The news had reached us that Frank Stagg, an Irish Republican prisoner from Hollymount, County Mayo had died in Wakefield Prison, England after 62 days on hunger strike demanding repatriation to Ireland!

We fought daily running battles with the local Protestant State School, Dunlambert, to the extent they staggered our starting and finishing times so we would not collide.

I left Bearnageeha and following a few years of unemployment I eventually trained and qualified as an Anaesthetic Technician at the Ulster Hospital at Dundonald. I was one of the few Catholic Nationalists to work there. After 16 years I left the Ulster and set up my own business as a Guest House proprietor in North Belfast, the epicentre of many of Belfast's sectarian killings and dubbed 'the murder mile'.

3,145 men and 321 females died in the conflict. 563 of those were in North Belfast. The total number injured was over 47,500 and included Police (*Royal Ulster Constabulary*), British Army Regular and Reserve *(Ulster Defence Regiment, a locally recruited protestant Militia)*, Republicans *(Irish Republican Army, Irish National Liberation Army, Official IRA)* Loyalist Paramilitaries *(Ulster Defence Association, Ulster Volunteer Force)* and Civilians.

Being born and reared in the sectarian cockpit of North Belfast, being stopped by Police and Soldiers, searched and questioned from a young age, I like many of my peers started to ask what was happening. Why did we have armed Police and Soldiers on our streets? Who, what, where and why did the Irish Republican movement exist, both Official and Provisional wings?

What were their goals? Why were Loyalist Paramilitaries murdering Catholics randomly on the streets and in their homes? Why was it not safe for me to walk more than three quarters of a mile in any direction from my front door, before it became dangerous territory, where I could be beaten, tortured or murdered? Why had men in cars tried to abduct me and a close friend from the streets near my home at the time the notorious Shankill Butchers were kidnapping, torturing and brutally murdering Catholics?

I was only 15 years of age.

The answers came as I grew older.

Ireland has a history of military and colonial occupation under the British. Ireland was Britain's first Colony. They then went on to colonise/ conquer/ occupy one quarter of the world's population without their permission, against their will, using superior weapons of war, terror, murder and torture to subdue foreign people in their own lands, for the exploitation of their resources: tea, opium, diamonds, coal, gold, tin, oil, cheap mass labour, slave labour and tax collection amongst others. Indeed they have invaded every country in the world on every continent, bar twenty two!

My country was divided, partitioned, against the will of the Irish people in 1921/22. A small proportion of the population, less than one fifth, descended from those Colonists drafted in from Scotland and England, who were settled here during the Plantation of Ulster to be loyal to England and who had been given the property and lands of the native indigenous Catholic Irish after they were ethnically cleansed from their ancestral homes and farms, now had a veto on the reunification of Ireland, having been given 6 counties, Antrim ,Down, Derry, Armagh, Fermanagh and Tyrone to rule as a one party pro-British Unionist State.

This new Unionist Government (in favour of the union with Britain) treated its Irish, Catholic, nationalist citizens here in a gerrymandered, sectarian, apartheid, bastardised state as second class citizens. We saw the plight and indeed the fight of the Blacks of America, the Blacks of South Africa and the Palestinians in the Middle East as our brothers and sisters in the universal call for justice, equality and self-determination.

I could write a whole book on the history of Britain's illegal occupation of my land but this book is about Palestine.

The struggle I saw on the streets of Belfast was one of a national war of independence against a foreign military and colonial occupation: a fight for reunification, for freedom, for justice and for equality. Those who had descended from the settler, who stole the land, had a right to live in harmony with the rest of us but not to prolong the injustice of partition on behalf of a foreign power, using sectarianism to divide and conquer the Irish people, much as it has done everywhere else the stained and bloody hand of British imperialism and colonisation has ruled.

1981 was a very tough time for Republican prisoners and their families and the attendant violence which accompanied the death of each of the ten hunger strikers was felt across our society, as death, disorder and destruction stalked our streets. These men died demanding Political Status, their actions those of resistance, of freedom fighters fighting against the criminalisation policy being pursued by the then British Prime Minister Margaret Thatcher. She gladly watched them die. After the hunger strike ended the men in Long Kesh Prison (*renamed the Maze*) were given de facto political status.

During the Hunger Strikes of 1981, I marched on some of the demonstrations demanding political status for Irish Republican Prisoners. At the age of 17 I, along with many others were becoming politicised thanks to Thatcher's right-wing policies: from Irish Republicans to the coal miners in Yorkshire.

I had been aware of the war of liberation being waged by the Palestine Liberation Organisation (PLO). I had heard of Yasser Arafat and Leila Khaled *(whom I met in Beirut in 2011)* and I saw murals showing a connection of comradely solidarity between the IRA and the PLO, two national liberation fronts, one struggle.

With this in mind, I remember hearing in 1982 that the Palestine Liberation Organisation was forced to withdraw from Beirut and disperse to Jordan, Syria, Iraq, Sudan, North and South Yemen, Tunisia and Greece. The new headquarters of the PLO would be in Tunisia. My first thought was why were the PLO in Beirut?

Ariel Sharon was the 'Butcher of Beirut': the war criminal who laid the plans for the massacres at Sabra and Shatila in the suburbs of Beirut in the refugee camps of the Palestinian diaspora. Israel had illegally invaded Lebanon with the purpose of displacing the PLO. They drove their war machine to the very heart of Beirut.

Once the PLO fighters had left under escort for Greece and beyond, an orgy of violence, murder, dismemberment and brutal killings were visited upon the young, the old, the sick, the feeble, the immobile and the vulnerable.

All in the name of a greater Israel carried out by the Christian Phalange Militias of Lebanon under the supervision and protection of Ariel Sharon, the Israeli Commander.

The Christian Phalange in Lebanon was a right wing, pro-French army, who spoke the colonial tongue of the French colonisers. Lebanon was once a French Colony, Beirut the Paris of the Middle East. The Phalange fought against the 'mainly Muslim Arab Lebanese and the mainly Muslim Arab PLO although many Palestinian Christians and seculars both fought for the PLO and the non-Phalange Lebanese Militias.

The Christian Phalange fought a debilitating civil war in Lebanon which benefitted France and Israel. The arrival of the PLO, having been driven out of Palestine in 1967 during the Six Day War, contributed to the instability of Lebanon whose Unity government exists today in a fragile coalition supported by Christians, Seculars and Muslims.

Sharon was the Defence Minister in the Israeli government who planned the invasion of Lebanon. He died in 2014 after a long illness following a debilitating stroke. 'Divine retribution' said some, 'not long enough' said others. A war criminal and mass murderer, I for one will never forget what he did to the defenceless men, women and children of Lebanon!

Between 6pm on September 16th to 8am on September 18th in 1982, between 762 and 3,500 civilians, mainly Palestinian and Lebanese Shiites, were murdered. The Phalanges, Maronite Christian militias, close allies of the Israelis, were ordered to clear the camps by the Israeli Defence Forces (IDF). The Israelis surrounded the camp, refused exit to the civilian population and lit the camps at night with flares so the massacres could continue all through the night.

From the turbulence in Belfast to massacres in Beirut I followed the news, read the papers, saw the plane hijackings and the ongoing violence but it was only in 2009 when I went onto Facebook that a whole new source of independent, non-governmental propagandised information was now at my disposal. That in turn led me to the media outlets, *Russia Today* and *Al Jazeera*.

I soon found like-minded people, many more educated than me in the affairs and the truth of what was happening in the Middle East and so a few fellow travellers came onto my radar and into my life.

As I sat in my living room in Parkview Lodge Guest House Belfast, with a new laptop used for the convenience of accepting and updating internet bookings and referrals, my new Toshiba, coupled with a lot of down time waiting for guests to arrive led to surfing the net and opening a Facebook account.

I had heard all the talk of Facebook being used by the big brother security services to spy, profile and target activists, stories which are undoubtedly true but the strength of Facebook and social media in general is that it does spread real news coverage, in real time by-passing the censors, who act for and on behalf of the establishment. I can read of Gaza being bombed by the Zionist Israelis literally within fifteen minutes of it happening. Social media has opened my eyes to the reality of how much our news coverage is biased, controlled and manipulated by our so called 'free press' at the behest of the small group of individuals who control our media and on behalf of our governments. The public narrative and the space occupied by the mainstream media are actually used to condition society to accept that which they want us to believe to be true. It is their view, not a world view, with all the inherent lies, deceit and propaganda that is attendant to it.

So, according to them, we have monarchies and dictatorships that are anti-democratic but compliant to western interests, usually American, and values that are 'good', such as Saudi Arabia, Jordan, Egypt and we have democratically elected governments like Hamas in Gaza or Allende in Chile and the Iranians pursuing their own political philosophy invading no-one and working for and on behalf of their electorate, and they are 'bad'!

Malcolm X said "If you're not careful, the newspapers will have you hating the people who are being oppressed, and loving the people who are doing the oppressing."

On Facebook I began to view posts on Palestine and Lebanon. I started reading comments, press releases, viewing video: I listened to inspiring singer songwriters such as the American David Rovics and Irish man Pol MacAdaim and English rapper Lowkey to hear of the sacrifice and martyrdom of Rachel Corrie a young American woman who died in Rafah in Gaza protecting a Palestinian home from demolition when the Israeli operated, American made and specially adapted for military use Caterpillar bulldozer, deliberately crushed young Rachel and even reversed over her.

When Rachel was in the 5th grade she gave a speech entitled "I'm here because I care".[1] I hope we realise her dream on how she wanted to see the world. Rachel was 23 when she was murdered on March 16 2003.

---

[1] https://youtu.be/pDq32EgMxb8

Tom Hurndall died on January 13th 2004 having been shot on April 11th 2003. A volunteer with the International Solidarity Movement (ISM) he was shot in the head by an Israeli soldier and sniper Taysir Hayb while in Gaza as a photographer and remained in a coma for nine months before eventually succumbing to his wounds. On April 10th 2006 a British inquest jury returned a verdict of unlawful killing. Tom's sister now works for Medical Aid for Palestine and his mum has written a book, *Defy The Stars: The life and death of Tom Hurndall*[2]. Tom was 23 when he was murdered.

There have been many ISM martyrs and many more wounded, including:

Australian Kate Edwards shot by Israeli forces in Beit Jala April 2nd 2002, *survived*

Irish woman Caoimhe Butterly shot and injured by Israeli Defence Forces in Jenin November 22nd 2002, *survived*

Rachel Corrie murdered in Rafah, crushed by an American made Caterpillar bulldozer deliberately driven over her by its Israeli operator March 16th 2003

American Brian Avery shot in the face April 5th 2003 *survived*

Britain Tom Hurndall shot April 11th 2003, died 9 months later of his injuries

American Tristan Anderson killed by a tear gas canister March 13th 2008

---

[2] Jocelyn Hurndall. *Defy The Stars: The Life and Death of Tom Hurndall*, (Bloomsbury UK, 2007)

Maltese Bianca Zammit shot in the thigh by IDF in Al Maghazi refugee camp May 31st 2010, *survived*

American Emily Henochowicz lost her eyesight in one eye having been injured by an IDF tear gas canister on May 31st 2010

Vittorio Arrigoni was killed by a militant Salafist group in Gaza On April 14th 2011

There are many other men and women who have stood in solidarity with the illegally militarily occupied people of Palestine of both the West Bank and Gaza, who have died or have been injured by the IDF. I do not know them all, nor have I met any of them personally with perhaps the exception being Vittorio Arrigoni whom I may have met in October 2010 in Gaza but I am not sure. To all those unpaid volunteers, paid non-governmental organisations, individuals and groups that have suffered, lost their lives, been injured, stood at protests, visited the region in solidarity, you have my unconditional love and support. Your sacrifice, bravery and steadfastness is a constant source of pride and encouragement for all those who realise that justice, freedom and equality for the oppressed will only end when we who have something, stand beside those who have nothing.

When men and women of goodwill stand idly by evil flourishes.

So if you have not yet become involved in the call for freedom with justice for Palestine, for self-determination and an end to the unconditional support for Israel's ongoing war crimes in the region, I would ask you to consider calling for Nationhood for Palestine, to include the right of return of Palestinian refugees to their homes in Palestine as enshrined in United Nations Resolution 194.

I remember attending a talk given in Belfast in the Grosvenor Hall, hosted by a local Palestine support group and given by a Holocaust survivor Hedy Epstein and also on the panel was a member of the Scottish Palestine support committee, Mick Napier.

On arrival we were asked to give a telephone number, email and or address for a follow up contact, to be placed on the email list. I made sure the people collecting this information were fully aware of my interest and desire to get involved and help but perhaps due to an administrative error, I never heard from them.

The talks were fantastic and to hear a Holocaust survivor denounce Israel's ethnic cleansing of Palestine was heart-warming and Mick's first-hand accounts of being in Palestine painted a powerful picture of what life under occupation sounded and felt like.

So I went back onto Facebook posting pictures of the talk, sharing information, learning more about the situation and the David and Goliath nature of the conflict.

Palestinians mainly unarmed or lightly armed were under siege and occupation by the fourth largest military force in the world. Israel armed, financed and politically supported by America's F16 fighter jets, Apache attack helicopters, tanks and a myriad of ships to include nuclear submarines.

Palestine has no army, no air force, no navy to defend it and no air raid shelters. Israel has all of these for its offensive destruction of Palestine. Palestinians have only their raw courage and the moral certainty of their just cause.

As we headed into Christmas 2008 here in Europe, I watched with dismay the attack on Gaza by the Israeli Government in Operation Cast Lead[3] and believe me, they cast plenty of it.

It was a sustained, brutal, murderous attack on the population of Gaza.

There are 1.8 million Palestinians living in Gaza in an area about 6 miles x 24 miles. The most densely populated area on the planet. Can you imagine a mass of humanity crammed into such a tiny

[3] Operation Cast Lead – December 27th 2008 – January 18th 2009

space subjected to violent attack? Many were already displaced refugees from 1948 at the creation of the state of Israel and again in 1967 from the Six Day War started by Israel with a pre-emptive strike on Egypt who they feared were building a military capacity that may eventually someday rival that of the Zionists. So tens of thousands having already been made homeless, jobless, sometimes parentless in these preceding events, were now under siege and under bombardment from earth, sea and sky: nowhere to run, nowhere to hide.

The war on Gaza began on December 27th 2008 and was completed on January 18th 2009. This military assault on the defenceless population included a land incursion by Israeli ground troops. The stated aim of the attacks was to destroy the home made rockets Hamas occasionally fired into Israel during times of tension as an almost futile response to Israeli military incursions, attacks on Gaza and the continued illegal siege placed on this coastal enclave. The Hamas rockets are basically rockets without a payload, the major damage they cause is akin to a small piece of metal falling from a plane and breaking roof tiles, damaging cars or making a crater in a road about the size of a football. Of course if you were physically hit by a small piece of metal falling from the sky it could kill you but as for payload while they are a great piece of engineering by the Palestinian resistance they are ineffective as a weapon of war.

The reality of Israel's war and its true objectives were obvious: bombing schools, mosques and hospitals, terrorising 1.8 million human beings devoid of bomb shelters, bereft of an early warning system. Just sheep hemmed into a pen being killed daily at will; no security, no defence, just defiance and resistance. Israel was bombing Gaza back into the middle ages.

Targeting hospitals, ambulances and places of education and worship are war crimes[4] against humanity.

By the time the Israelis had spent their American stockpile of weapons and bombed everything they could, Gaza had lost up to 1,419 of its sons and daughters, fathers and mothers, brothers and sisters, friends and neighbours of which at least 308 were children and 253 were women.[5]

On that fateful morning at 11.30am F16 Fighter jets, Apache helicopters and unmanned Drones simultaneously bombed and destroyed over one hundred separate targets including a police cadet graduation ceremony without warning. The police academy and its recruits are seen everywhere in the world as part of the civilian administration, distinct and separate from the army. Not if you're Israeli and part of the Zionist government. They deliberately murdered over 99 police graduates and 9 civilians who were attending their graduation ceremony; they targeted police stations and at the end of the first day over 230 Palestinians were in the morgue.

The Samouni family lost 21 members of their extended family, all civilians. Israeli soldiers forced the extended family of about 100 members into one building and 24 hours later shelled them.

The Al Daya family lost 22 members, nearly all women and children who had huddled together for safety before their home was hit by a F16 missile.

White phosphorous was used in Israeli ammunitions to mortar and bomb Gaza. It is illegal under international law to use it in populated areas. The phosphorus burns right to the bone once it has made contact with the skin.

---

[4] The Hague Conventions of 1899,1907 & 1954 outlined the rules of war.(It is illegal to attack a defenseless person or place; it is illegal to attack a building that is being used as a hospital)

[5] Palestinian Centre for Human Rights

3,500 homes destroyed, a further 2,870 damaged, more than 20,000 people left homeless, $10,000,000 of damage caused to the Gaza electricity infrastructure.

268 private businesses destroyed and 432 damaged, 107 United Nations Relief and Works Agency (UNRWA) installations damaged.

18 schools destroyed, 262 damaged.

Over 85% of those murdered by Israel were civilian non-combatants.

Over 1,400 dead and over 5,000 injured.

13 Israelis died, 4 by friendly fire and 182 were injured when Hamas and the resistance responded to the Israeli attacks with 750 mortars and rockets.

So there we have it. Superior military might by Israel coupled with a distinct lack of morality contrived to create another massacre against a relatively defenceless people, corralled, with no shelter, no means of escape and no security.

It was just another chapter in the Zionist Book of War Crimes.

Protests were held on the streets of Belfast, Dublin, London, Glasgow and across many cities, towns and villages throughout the world.

Ethnic cleansing, genocide, mass murder, call it what you will, I call it Israeli governmental policy towards the indigenous population of Palestine, it is as inhuman as it is unforgivable.

All colonial and imperialist occupations are the same. Where-ever possible wipe out the natives, control their movement, steal their land, resources and power, deny them access to education, prosecute them in the courts and make them cower in their homes, force them to accept the occupation through military and judicial brutality.

To see how Palestinians have suffered, just look at the native tribes of the Americas, 100 million murdered, killed and starved to death by white European settlers, India under the British, Mexico under the Americans and Algeria under the French. Aborigines were treated as 'Flora and Fauna' under Australian law with no rights under the constitution right up until the 1960s.

Israel is a predominantly white European colony, superimposed upon the land of Palestine, a land they have stolen and where they have created a racist, apartheid, Jewish only state. It was built and continues to be built on the broken dreams, broken homes and broken bones of the indigenous people of Palestine.

Israel's aim? A greater Israel, manufactured by dispossessing all of Palestine from its people and absorbing land from neighbouring territory such as the occupied Syria Golan Heights. Israel is the only country in the world that refuses to define its borders as it seeks to graft itself onto neighbouring Arab lands.

Operation Cast Lead became a catalyst for many who oppose the Zionist occupation of historic Palestine and the continuing illegal military and colonial settler occupation of the West Bank of the occupied Palestinian Territories and the ongoing immoral and inhuman siege of Gaza.

From demonstrations in all the major cities across the globe to burgeoning fledgling support from individuals and a renaissance of many of the long established Palestine advocacy groups, Israel's barbarism has created the BDS movement and has awakened in many, the desire for peace in the Middle East and peace for Palestine.

Israel wants piece, in fact it wants every piece of Palestine it can get.

Contrary to the Zionist mantra that Palestinians and the Arab/Persian collective are the problem in the region, it is Israel and its pseudo supporters in western governments, many fundamentalist Christians and some who worship at the altar of money, or to get re-elected, who finance, arm and give political cover to the atrocities carried out by the Israeli government, including extra judicial murders and assassinations of those who they believe pose a threat to Israel's security be they Palestinian, Iranian, Lebanese, Iraqi, Syrian, Egyptian, Libyan or other.

After all Britain allowed the migration to Palestine of European Jews and Zionists. America gave them the technology to grow an arsenal of up to 400 nuclear weapons.

As we leave January 2009 and the massacre of Gaza we head towards the attempts by many to end, break, or highlight internationally the siege of Gaza.

There were several attempts to deliver medical aid and supplies to Gaza by sea involving small boats carrying several tons per sailing. The first voyage was in August 2008 followed again in December 2008, June 2009 then May 2010.

The first two arrived successfully and it appeared a chink in Israel's siege of Gaza had been found but then the Israeli navy began to intercept militarily these humanitarian deliveries of wheelchairs, surgical instruments, penicillin, blood plasma, bandages and arrested the people who were risking their lives to deliver this much needed, life-saving aid. Many were international journalists and activists, some like Mairead Corrigan Maguire were Nobel Prize winners, others Holocaust survivors.

Let's fast forward to May 2010 and the sailing of a Freedom Flotilla organised by among others the Free Gaza Movement, The International Solidarity Movement and the Turkish Humanitarian Relief Foundation (IHH).

I'd been sharing posts on Facebook about Palestine and met similarly minded individuals. We met up at an anti-racism function in West Belfast. There were initially five of us including my partner Pauline and we discussed the possible fate of the flotilla, expressed our support and wondered what we should do to highlight this latest attempt to get aid to those in need in Gaza. The result of the siege meant medical supplies, medicines and fuel to run the electricity generators were in short supply and in effect people were dying needlessly every week due to lack of basic utilities such as clean water and sanitation.

We decided collectively that the most likely outcome of the flotilla was that it would be hijacked illegally in international waters of the coast of Gaza by Israel and all those involved arrested and taken to the Israeli port of Ashdod.

There was an Irish ship taking part in the flotilla called the *Rachel Corrie* named after the young American activist murdered in Gaza. The flotilla was due to reach these international waters off Gaza in the early morning of May 31st 2010.

The Belfast branch of the Irish Palestine Support Committee was attending a national vigil demonstration in Dublin and we decided the people in Belfast should be offered the opportunity to show their support in castigating Israel for intercepting the flotilla. Five of us called a protest rally outside Belfast City Hall on Bank Holiday Monday, May 31st 2010.

I had followed the flotilla on the internet as they navigated the dangerous trip towards Gaza. One of the last messages I read was Israeli warships were on the horizon and the flotilla was being challenged and threatened with being boarded. This was piracy on the high seas. A humanitarian aid convoy which had been searched and passed customs in Turkey was being hijacked and the people kidnapped by armed Israeli Commandos from high speed boats and attack helicopters.

Once communication from the ships was broken and being about 4am in the morning I fell asleep. When I awoke I began to read reports that the flotilla had indeed been intercepted as we had feared but also worryingly some of the crew and participants may have been injured or killed.

When we arrived at the City Hall expecting a handful of activists there must have been over 300 people from the Trade Union movement, local political parties and concerned individuals with Palestine Flags and banners. The media were in attendance along with Patricia McKeown, President of the Trade Union *Unison* and Gerry Adams, President of Sinn Fein, an elected abstentionist Irish Republican Member of the British Parliament for West Belfast.

Being conscious of the fact we were a small group of individuals with no elected mandate, as spokesperson for the group on the day I asked if Mr Adams would like to address the crowd. To their credit, Sinn Féin declined. "Your group called the protest, you should speak". I went on to read a short prepared statement to those assembled and invited others to speak including Dr Saeb Shaath a former Palestinian representative to Ireland.

The protest was successful and we decided to try to keep the momentum going and called for another protest the following week. From this small initial gathering of five we formed a Palestinian support group and went on to raise monies via a fundraiser, the proceeds of which were forwarded to the Irish Medical Aid for Palestine Charity based in Dublin.

During a live link up via skype with the Al Awda hospital in Gaza city and chilling out and having a chat with Dr Saeb Shaath from Gaza, he suddenly said, "Fra, it is great to raise money and support the hospital by transferring funds electronically but real solidarity is going physically to stand by the people, shoulder to shoulder". That had a profound effect on me and the seed had been planted. I ruminated on what had been said I had to agree with Saeb it was time to walk the walk.

Tony Upton (another Group member) and I made a commitment to join the 'Viva Palestina Medical Aid' convoy to Gaza organised by George Galloway, a personal hero of mine.

George Galloway is an absolute icon of mine because of his stance on Palestine, Kashmir and Ireland. He speaks his truth, which I share and is a noble exponent of humanity and socialism. He has his detractors and haters and probably might have done some things differently, as we might all do but as a man of conscience when he speaks I hear my own thoughts, while he may well speak for himself he is the voice of the voiceless.

Many people helped with our fundraising effort including those with whom we had formed a fledgling support group and Dr Saeb Shaath helped in the initial fundraiser.

I was a bit reluctant at first to leave my comfort zone, leave home for a road trip with a group of strangers and go to a place that was regularly being bombed. Having survived a violent conflict in my own country for 25 years I was aware more than many of the possible outcomes from being injured to being killed, a very slim possibility but not one to be discounted lightly.

Within days of deciding to go we had joined the Viva Palestina volunteer register, applied for international driving licenses, paid our registration fees and tried to meet up with others who were going.

Inside six weeks, fundraisers had been organised and help including very generous donations by the people of the Clonard Catholic Church in West Belfast helped us source a mini bus on Ebay from two guys in Wales.

It's amazing how things come together. Initial telephone calls with the sellers agreed they would drive the vehicle to the docks in

Holyhead in Wales and Tony and I would go to Dublin, take the ferry over, pay for the vehicle and then bring it back.

On hearing of our plan to deliver medical aid to Palestine they offered to bring the van to Dublin and two days before confirmation of our purchase they delivered it to my front door on the Cavehill Road in Belfast.

To their eternal credit and after a few worried phone calls looking for directions the guys arrived with the minibus, refused an offer to stay overnight, refused to accept petrol money for their journey or the boat crossing and insisted they only wanted the price agreed for the original pick up in Wales. Fair play lads, Tony and I never forgot your generosity and I hope you are both well.

By this stage Tony and I had separated from the support group believing it was being taken over covertly by a local political grouping so to all intents and purposes it was now just us.

We had about two weeks to go before the convoy was due to leave London early in September. We had been advised by the organisers to contact John Hurson, a native of Dungannon in County Tyrone in the North of Ireland, as he was organising the Irish participation on the convoy. John suggested a meeting at a petrol station forecourt in Dublin airport so two guys from Tipperary in Southern Ireland, two guys from Ballycastle in the North of Ireland and two guys from Belfast could all meet up and spend half an hour with the Patron of Viva Palestina who was in Ireland for a few days.

Tony and I jumped in the van, drove to the airport and were introduced to Joe Gilmartin and Seamus from Tipperary Padraig (paudy) McShane and John from Ballycastle, John Hurson from Dungannon and none other than the mighty George Galloway himself. It was a momentous meeting, George smoking his usual cigars probably Cuban, signing our tee shirts and welcoming us on the journey to Palestine.

There is no greater motivator than meeting an icon you admire. It was a pivotal moment and enthused us for the trials and tribulations that lay ahead.

With nearly everything in place just two things remained. Getting decals for the van and telling the people you love your off to a war zone. We found a vehicle graphics firm in West Belfast and proclaimed to the world we were 'Belfast to Gaza'.

On one side of the minibus Tony put the quote by Bobby Sands IRA hunger striker and Member of Parliament for Fermanagh South Tyrone, *Our revenge will be the laughter of our children*. On the other side I had placed the lyrics of a fine American Jewish singer songwriter David Rovics *Tell the children of Jerusalem they are not alone*.

That was the easy bit done. Fundraising completed, van organised, and medical aid in the back of minibus, bandages, walking frames, wheelchairs, now just to tell the family.

Everything had been pretty hectic, just six short weeks from contacting the organisers of the Viva Palestina Aid Convoy and even though some of the family knew I was fundraising with others to get to Gaza it was never a reality until everything was in place. I did not actually think we would complete the plan I just put my head down and went for it.

My brother Eric was over from England visiting my mum. We had a mutual family friend named Steven Scott and his wife Patricia who invited us for dinner. Lasagne was on the menu and Gaza in my thoughts. That night is etched forever in my mind.

Eric, my partner Pauline and I headed down to Stephen and Patricia's home in Newington, North Belfast for dinner. Half way through the evening during a lull in the conversation while all the time my mind was preoccupied on the trip ahead I said to Pauline, "well, should I tell them"? Truth be told I was putting it off as I knew the reaction I would most likely receive.

I took a deep breath and said "I am going to Gaza".

Stunned silence! Followed by "are you sure you want to do that"? "Is that not where people are getting killed"? I told them about the convoy, expressed my view that real solidarity work comes with a price tag and true empathy comes from standing shoulder to shoulder with those under occupation, oppressed and discriminated against. We had a toast to Palestine and the trip ahead and I finally felt a sense of relief, like a guilty sin had been confessed. A purpose was born and reaffirmed that night, a determination come what may to see it through.

A second conversation followed at home with my mum who wished me good luck and asked that I contact home as often as possible while I was away. A farewell to my sister Ursula, brothers Conor and Chris and D day was fast approaching.

Although my partner Pauline was the manager of the Parkview Lodge Bed and Breakfast we had bought I couldn't just take off for an unspecified, prolonged journey without her love and support. The night before we were due to go to London to join the convoy Pauline, her friend Jane and I went for food at Soprano's Pizzeria on the Antrim Road. We knew most of the staff and ate there on a regular basis. Half way through the meal as we talked about the trip with Jane, Pauline started crying. One of the staff came over to ask if she was ok. We explained to her that I was going to Palestine, to Gaza. She started crying too. It became apparent that no-one knew, including me, if I would be coming back. I could be hurt during the journey which entailed a prolonged drive through Europe, parts of Africa and the Middle East. I could be injured or killed in Gaza as the Zionists were bombing the coastal enclave almost every week.

23

It was maybe the first time I realised or appreciated how much Pauline loved me and indeed how much she would worry and be anxious for my safety.

Those who wait at home also suffer.

Mrs Ursula Patrica Hughes nee McSwiggan

Belfast To Gaza

September -October 2010

Chapter 2

The following day September 22nd 2010 I picked up Tony Upton my companion and comrade on this epic journey and headed for a brief stop at Belfast City Hall where it had been suggested that we set off from to be waved off by a few well-wishers. My brother Chris was there, Dr Saeb Shaath, some of Tony's family and a few friends of mine including 'Mols' aka Paul Mulally.

The Police were pretty quick to try and move us on but we ignored them for a good 20-30 minutes, then three times round the Dome of Delight as our City Hall is affectionately known and off on the rocky road to Dublin to meet the Boys

This quick rundown the motorway was the first time we had road tested the vehicle and the really first time people had an opportunity to see the van. Plastered in Palestinian and Irish flags Belfast to Gaza, we got a few strange looks and varied reactions.

While Ireland is perceived to be fairly sympathetic to the cause of Palestine with our very own ongoing military occupation by the British, there are some pro-Zionist, neo-Christian fundamentalists along with fascists who support the right wing, no matter where they are. Funny how racists and fascists hate Jews, Blacks and Catholics yet support Zionism? Go figure.

We arrived in Dublin in good order and in good time to meet the guys who were to become our travel companions and good friends on the perilous road ahead.

Paudy and John from Ballycastle, Joe and Seamus from Tipperary, Fra and Tony from Belfast - The Irish Crew: all Irishmen, all politically aware activists, all deeply moved by the plight of the whole Palestinian people living under repression, injustice and illegal military occupation.

Finally I felt at home!

We found ourselves on the deck of the Dublin to Holyhead ferry on a cold September evening watching the stars glitter on a cloudless night over the Irish Sea. A beer or two, some friendly inconsequential small talk, as we didn't really know each other but it was really great to see three vans one 'Tipp To Gaza' , one 'Antrim To Gaza' and one 'Belfast To Gaza'. It made my heart swell with pride and it still does, Irishmen showing the Children of Jerusalem they are not alone.

After a few hours of broken sleep, I showered, had breakfast, jumped into the van and off the boat, on the road to a warehouse in London. Finally, after weeks of preparation the Odyssey had begun.

The traffic became chaotic as you can imagine the closer we drew to London and with the nights beginning to draw in it was dark before our sat nav directed us to where the vehicles were to be secured overnight and where we would meet, for the first time, some of our other fellow travellers, the Viva Palestina convoy of 2010, to include our British Muslim brothers and sisters, other European, Canadian, New Zealand, Australian and American compatriots but more of that later.

The Irish lads had all procured their own vehicles through various channels but the Malaysian and those from outside the UK had relied on Viva Palestina to purchase vehicles on their behalf. When we arrived these vehicles were having the decals fitted to identify which country they were representing. Some convoy members had signed up alone and were being teamed up with other single drivers, always two per vehicle to share the driving and of course there is always a bus that acts as the general headquarters and can carry several people so it allows for companionship and comradery.

I can still recall the buzz in the warehouse whose services had been donated free. I remember the sense of brotherhood, of working together to load the medical aid and check the oil, tyre pressures, water levels - the introductions, the different exotic names and the different cultural values on display.

We had not booked any accommodation and as more people were due to arrive the next day we wondered if we should we sleep in the vans, after all, that was part of the plan when we hit the road, campsites and cheap motels and cooking at the side of the road would be the order of the day!

A young British Muslim guy, most likely having family back in Pakistan, asked us where we staying. We told him we had not arranged anything and ten minutes later he came back to us with a set of keys and directions to a nearby house. So the six of us and a few others set off down the road, grabbed food, a few beers and we slept on the beds, the sofas and the floors.

Another exciting but restless night and we hadn't even left London.

Next day at the warehouse we were informed that the convoy would travel to the embankment near the House of Commons for a send-off and press coverage with George Galloway, our Patron, and perhaps the visionary behind the convoy ideas. As the day progressed we began to hear concerns that the English Defence League among others were planning a very different kind of reception and send off for us, so plans were drawn up mainly by those on the convoy as to how to react to any violent attack from the Fascists in Britain. We had Irish and we had Muslims, both high value targets for these right wing thugs who had publicly threatened us.

The decision was made. Half the convoy was to go to the send-off with George Galloway, the other half to wait on us at a service station en route to the channel tunnel.

The Irish guys got together; we decided to keep handy some Irish hurling bats also referred to as Hurley sticks. We put on our newly acquired Viva Palestina Convoy tee shirts (only 45 issued in London for members of the convoy) and joined formation with the other vehicles.

I put on some Rebel music, Tony put out the Irish Tricolour and the Palestinian Flag and we headed for the Embankment determined to face what may come. We arrived incident free at the press conference and George gave a rousing speech endorsing the humanitarian nature of the convoy, wished us God's speed and promised to join us on the journey. We left for the rendezvous point, wary of an ambush or attack as we were quite vulnerable from stone throwing while driving but nothing materialised - typical fascist cowards.

When we met at the service station some guys got out a football, we got out a hurl and a slither (a small leather bound ball similar to a cricket ball) and passed the afternoon in the sunshine while awaiting our departure time to Paris, France for the next stage on our planned itinerary.

I think it was on the first day I met Colin from Belfast who had travelled separately to rest of the Irish, John Hurson one of the convoy organisers from Dungannon in Co. Tyrone in the North of Ireland, Mark from Liverpool and Carole Swords from London. Was it day two or three on the convoy, sure hadn't I lost count already?

All I knew was we were going to Palestine, to Gaza and everyone seemed dead on, really helpful, nice and of a similar mind set. Of course as we got to know each other, each individual story, the rationale behind it became clearer, but at this moment in time I was enjoying the companionship and the tolerance people display when getting to know each other.

So off we went on a glorious September afternoon, convoy style, heading for Europe and the epic journey that awaited us. Roll on the suburbs of Paris where we were meant to stay.

As we headed into France it became apparent how difficult convoy driving might be become. We had been assigned call signs, vehicle numbers and walkie talkies for each section of the convoy. We had Alpha, Bravo and Charlie sections and where possible people were kept together to help build bonds and comradeship. Tony, I and the Irish Brigade as we were now known, all ended up in Charlie Company with some of our Muslim Brothers from Birmingham, Bradford and London. The Pakkies and the Paddies as John Hurson called us.

C1 at the front had a walkie talkie and C10 at the back had a walkie talkie and everyone in between had to just sit on the bumper of the vehicle in front. It sounds ok but when someone heads off like a bat out of hell then we are all driving at the fastest speed to keep up and we had a few worrying moments along the Rue de Paris.

I remember entering one of tunnels en route to Paris, hammering along the road when I saw a broken down van in one lane directly ahead of me. Now for anyone who has experienced driving in Europe it can feel like it's everyman for himself. To approach a stationary vehicle at speed in traffic with the lanes beside you fully occupied can seem daunting so it was on the horn, brake, accelerate, pull out and overtake. The real scary thing is the guy with the stationary vehicle has popped the bonnet and was busy pouring water into an over-heated engine. To say this was very

29

dangerous would be an understatement. To say the van involved was one of ours would be correct. An overheating engine that would require regular unplanned stops on the way to Gaza was something I had not accounted for.

As we rolled into the suburbs of Paris, to where we were being hosted and billeted for the night, we discovered a hearty welcome, hot food and lots of solidarity and well wishes. Arab cuisine and French hospitality saw us park our vehicles in the allotted car park, mingle with our hosts, head out for a beer and return to sleep on the floor of a gymnasium. Our first night on the road in Paris was an amalgamation of activists with different cultural values, different languages, bedding down on the floor in stairwells and in the gym with sleeping bags and pillows.

We discovered one of those greeting us was the Mayor of this Suburb of Paris and they had twinned the municipality with Sabra and Shatilla refugee camps in Beirut, Lebanon. That suited me right down to the ground, no better company than that.

The following morning breakfast was supplied, eggs, humus, cereal, baguettes, butter, hot coffee and pastries. Tony and a few others were passing time outside with the hurling stick and the ball when he tripped on a divot on the grass and twisted his knee. As my co-pilot and co-driver we decided he would ride shotgun until his knee was better.

We headed off for central Paris with a fanfare of horns and flags and a sea of smiling faces as we drove around the major attractions in the city centre. The plan was to raise awareness around the convoy and its stated mission to deliver aid and solidarity to the besieged people of Gaza, Palestine. We drove around the Bastille, the Arc de Triomphe and along the boulevards, we stopped, took photos and sang chants:

ONE TWO THREE FOUR,
OCCUPATION NO MORE,
FIVE SIX SEVEN EIGHT,
ISRAEL IS A TERRORIST STATE,
FROM THE RIVER TO THE SEA,
PALESTINE WILL BE FREE!

Many applauded us, some joined in for both photographs and the chants and several gave donations. One old man, a Palestinian living in France, gave us money and shed tears saying 'God bless you on your journey to Palestine'. We could travel as foreigners to the land of his birth, a journey Israel had refused him to complete as a refugee forced from his homeland, never to be allowed to return. We shed a few tears ourselves. What kind of a world did we inherit when old men cannot return home for a visit to see family and friends, visit graves and remember their youth?

A never forgotten afternoon in the capital of France but alas like all good things it came to an end. Paris wasn't our destination, just a stop off point.

Tanks refuelled both vehicle and tummies we were back on the road. Where to next?

Each morning and each evening on the convoy we had a meeting to review the day, to see how people were doing collectively, vehicle problems, reports and an itinerary of the day ahead. These meetings were essential for the smooth running of our project and helped solidify group dynamics and engagement.

Late in the afternoon we headed for Lyon and another dash down the motorways of Europe. Tony had pledged to fly the two national flags, the Irish tricolour and the Flag of Palestine, from our vehicle. A strong person both physically and mentally, Tony stuck to his promise even at 80 miles per hour as he held the two symbols of our entwined struggles together out the window wedged between hands and legs, he proudly let everyone who saw us on the road know who we were and what we stood for. I will always have that memory of Tony emblazoned on my mind. I'm so proud of that man, he made my heart soar.

Music on, David Rovics and Irish rebel tunes, I was fast beginning to cherish two songs in particular, *Aidan McAnespie* about a young unarmed man gunned down by a British Soldier who shot him on his way to a Gaelic Athletic football ground. An aimed shot at 200 metres from a machine gun, cutting him down and taking his life and *A song for Marcella*, a beautiful haunting song about IRA hunger striker Bobby Sands who died in Long Kesh prison after 66 days on Hunger Strike. An Irish republican, in a British jail, on Irish soil, denied the right to be treated as a political prisoner, criminalised by Margaret Thatcher. Bobby Sands was the first of ten men to die in the struggle for decriminalisation and to attain political status in the jail. Added to Rovics songs *They're building a wall, Jennin, All aboard the Mavi Marmara* plus the fantastic weather, the road trip was going really well.

In Lyon we drove again out to our rendezvous point at a campsite and we then took some of the vehicles into Lyon for a reception in the town square. Again we were greeted by TV crews, local officials, Arabs, Palestinians, French socialists, Anarchists and others wishing us well on our journey. We were joined by a French national who was bringing building supplies to Gaza to help rebuild a destroyed home.

Each evening we sought out an internet café with a Wi-Fi point so we could all contact friends and family at home. I was in daily contact with my partner Pauline and I asked her to relay to the rest of the family that I was in good spirits and that all was well.

I didn't realise just how many people were interested in and following our progress on our Belfast To Gaza Facebook page and even years later I meet people who say 'hey you went to Gaza' and

I reply 'yes on the Viva Palestina Aid Convoy with George Galloway in 2010' and they would say 'yeah I followed you online, great job Fra'.

George Galloway was busy in London and not able to go on the arduous daily road trip to Gaza. What he did and did well was to come and join us on the road and lead us whenever he could. He was in Paris to greet us when we arrived and I would have the chance to sit and have lunch with him before we had completed our trip. We talked about Palestine and we started to engage more with the other convoy members so I got to know firstly the rest of Charlie Company and by extension everyone else.

I met Waheed, Mansoor, Ron McKay, Tony the bus driver, Carole Swords, a good friend all British, Azra Banu from Malaysia and some people from America. I was never home sick as our days were full and our minds occupied. The convoy was well run and everyone was talking about the end journey Gaza and whether or not we would be allowed entry via Egypt. There is no way the convoy could have gone through Jordan to the Allenby crossing with Israel and then via the Erez crossing to Gaza. The Zionists would simply not allow any aid medical supplies or solidarity activists to show human concern for those suffering under their brutal Zionist sanctions, which is in effect what the siege is about. A siege as in the medieval days is designed to bring those under siege under the control, will and direction of those exercising the siege.

So it was to be Egypt via the Rafah border crossing but only with the consent of the Egyptian dictator Mubarak.

It was only on the road that I heard of the violence visited upon a previous Viva Palestina Convoy in the port of El Arish, Egypt when the convoy was attacked by Egyptian security personnel with many hurt and injured with several who required medical intervention and hospitalisation. Indeed George Galloway who led the convoy amongst others, was persona non grata in Egypt and could not even enter the country.

So we still had thousands of miles to go before we could reach our destination. We had to negotiate with the Egyptians to enter Egypt and then to enter Gaza and we still faced an uncertain fate during our stay in the besieged coastal enclave which was routinely bombed by Israel with many being killed and injured.

But best not to think of that -one day at a time, each day nearer to our destination, moving closer to our goal. Let those in charge sort out the finer details. My attitude was stick to the plan, drive until someone said stop and keep up my spirits and those around me.

Tony and I were doing well. The journey was tiring, a lot of miles to cover each day, a lot of concentration and a lack of sleep each evening due to communal sleeping arrangements and hard surfaces to lie on was having an effect but we were getting there. Fresh conversations each night, a stroll, a beer or coffee, food and a few treats like contacting home kept us going.

Now we headed over the mountains and into Italy.

Leaving Belfast City Hall for Gaza, September 2010

A great start

Chapter Three

The road to Italy was nothing less than spectacular, a sea of vehicles heading over the mountains, breath taking and majestic. As we arrived in Italy at the border crossing we were met by a television crew working for Al Jazeera who interviewed me and Tony as we awaited the arrival of some of our companions.

Sherif Fahy, originally from Cairo, Egypt now living and working in Rome, had driven to the border crossing to cover the story and indeed accompanied us through our days in Italy. We headed towards Turin where we would meet and be joined by a group of Italian activists who would complete the European component of the convoy and in the process become good friends.

We all set off re-energised and more upbeat. There were about 12 to 15 Italians in total, I am not sure if they were communists, anarchists or socialists but they were very welcome.

There was a huge reception again with food, assorted press and well-wishers in Turin and another night under canvas.

Milan next and the Duomo, the Cathedral which would challenge any other in the world. I had been in Italy on vacation before and visited Milan, a beautiful city, another Wi-Fi café and contact with home, some nice Italian food and whoosh, off to the Italian port of Ancona where Sherif asked Tony and I to go to the back of the ship and wave our flags as the boat set sail for an overnight ferry to Thessalonica in Greece. Little did I suspect that I would meet Sherif and his beautiful wife in Belfast many years later when he was filming a documentary on the walls of division/separation in Palestine/Israel, Greek /Turkish Cyprus and Belfast's inimitable peace walls between British settlers and the Indigenous Irish.

Between being on the road, nights of interrupted sleep, new convoy members and the fact that Tony was as yet unrecovered from his knee injury, I was beginning to tire. I nearly fell asleep behind the wheel on more than one occasion but we arrived safely in Greece and stayed in a camping site by the sea.

The very first thing to do after parking the van up for the night was to run down to the beach and have a swim. About half a dozen of us raced to the water's edge like school kids or young friends, carefree and adventurous, we jumped in. Cold yet inviting it revitalised us. We headed into town for dinner. What a beautiful town. I can understand the attraction and love affairs people have with Italy and Greece. The culture, the food, the wine, the sunshine and sun dappled lanes and boulevards are mesmerising. I was beginning to enjoy the trip for the travel and adventure it was affording me.

The following day we drove in convoy around Thessalonica blaring horns, waving flags, playing our music and generally raising the roof. The people were great and then back on the road. Each day we travelled for maybe ten hours, usually arriving late in the evening, have a welcome meeting with those hosting us and securing our accommodation, a race round the town and then onto our next port of call. The routine was good and each day brought us nearer to our objective. We were heading to Turkey where our vehicle insurance would expire, as we left Europe and entered Asia and the Middle East. We would need to secure insurance for each country we would now pass through and that included getting visas at the border and customs check points.

Turkey was eye-opening.

We were met by IHH Humanitarian Relief Foundation, a non-governmental organisation which carried out Charitable work all over the world and who were the people behind the Mavi Marmara, the medical aid ship that was so brutally attacked by Zionist killers in international waters and our inspiration for beginning this journey.

We had a prolonged wait at the border for several hours, where we gathered around in the midday sun, wandering about and discussing the delay until we finally got through, I will never forget the greeting. Hundreds were there to meet us.

Again, there were TV crews and associated press, Al Jazeera, local press, local TV companies and a huge welcome. Flags, bottles of water, food, hugs, kisses, a real outpouring of humanity. Considering several members of IHH had been murdered on the Mavi Marmara, The Shaheeds, the martyrs, I was over awed to be in their company.

They reset the formation, gave us an escort and we traversed the toll booths on the road to Istanbul. We entered the city and were brought to a beautiful restaurant with a view of the Bosphorous which divides East and West Istanbul and also divides Europe from Asia. We were made to feel very welcome and joined the members of IHH for food and entertainment. This was one of my favourite nights on the road. Twenty Five million people live in Istanbul and to see it lit up at night teeming with life was exceptional.

The next day we would visit the Blue Mosque for a press conference then have lunch by the river and this is where George Galloway rejoined the convoy and had lunch with us. As he entered the restaurant he walked up to the table I was sitting at, I moved aside and he sat down. That's when I met the real George Galloway - another activist, humble, sincere, down to earth, erudite and interesting. I was in awe of this great orator and yet he made me feel comfortable and relaxed in his company.

One hour I will always treasure, so much so I canvassed for him on two occasions; once in Bradford when he won the seat as MP and the second time when he lost to a resurgent Labour. George is on Press TV and many other TV channels, has his own show, is respected and admired by leaders on the left throughout the world and always, always, always has the interests of the working class people at the forefront of his politics, as he stands up to hypocrisy, imperialism, capitalism and war mongering. You just gotta love that man. I know I do!

As I had been getting to know my Muslim brothers and sisters on the convoy I had no reservations when some of the guys asked me to join them in prayer in the Blue Mosque. I washed my hands, feet, ears, mouth, neck and nostrils, slipped off my shoes and stepped inside the mosaic and grandiose old mosque of Istanbul. I can appreciate architectural beauty anywhere and while religion is not an interest of mine, I can see the power of positive love, as opposed to the controlling nature of organised religion.

We stayed in a hotel and had time to visit the markets, a short stop over to recharge the batteries, then onto a hotel in the mountains near the Syrian border.

We visited the grave of Furkan Dogan, a member of IHH. Dogan was a young Turkish American Doctor whose dream was to go to Africa and restore people's sight following blinding cataracts. A dream he would never realise as he was murdered unarmed on his way to Gaza with medical aid on board the Mavi Marmara. I was truly blessed to be given the opportunity to pay tribute to his sacrifice as, with several others, I gave an oration at his graveside with his family in attendance and our words being translated. I paid tribute to his courage and said how I was inspired by his heroism to go on the convoy and while he may have died, many others including me, would pick up the torch of humanity he had laid down and continue his fight to see freedom and justice for the people of Palestine.

A vision I hope to realise in my lifetime.

We headed onto a hotel in the mountains which in the winter was used as a ski resort but was mothballed in late September when we arrived. I met Mustafa Dogan, Furkans brother and although he had no English and I had no Turkish we attempted to communicate about Furkan. I will never forget that meeting nor indeed the deep sense of loss and sadness he conveyed on his brother's death. Small things and chance meetings can have a profound impact on us. I will never forget Furkans courage nor meeting Mustafa and who knows, we may well meet again.

How many days now?
How many countries?
I was beginning to lose count. Belfast, Dublin, London, Paris, Lyon, Turin, Milan, Ancona, Thessalonika, Istanbul, Ankara and now for Syria the last stop en route to Palestine.

So many things in such a short time I had no real time to evaluate them.

Again the delays on the Turkish Syrian border leaving Turkey were similar to the delays entering Turkey but if we thought we had a unrivalled welcome from IHH, the reception in Syria with ministers of State, Generals, Officials and Dignitaries is something I will probably never witness again. There were so many people to meet us that we had to abandon our vehicles and mingle with those gathered. We were ushered into a huge structure, a marquee to find shelter from the overhead sun. The convoy members were distributed out among the assembled guests, given food, water, soft drinks and welcome gifts and from the podium opposite welcome speeches were being relayed. I was beginning to get a bit restless, after all we had travelled so far, been on the road for several days and I didn't want to sit cooped up. Then I noticed Tony standing on the main road with our Belfast To Gaza flag. There and then I thought, the reception was magnificent but here's my friend and comrade and I wanted to be standing with him listening to the speeches, not with strangers no matter how hospitable and welcoming they were, so I made my excuses and then made my way onto the road in front of the podium beside Tony. Within minutes all the convoy members and many of the guests had left their seats and a second impromptu celebration was underway.

I was later told that when other convoy members saw me get up they followed suit and at one stage some Syrians, singing, hoisted me onto their shoulders and carried me aloft for several minutes.

A remarkable festival and out pouring of shared love is the only way I can describe it.

As the afternoon wore on it became apparent that the daylight was fading and we still had several hours travel ahead of us, before we would reach what was to become our home in Syria. So with fond farewells, a police escort and with the sun now slowly setting on the horizon, amid a blaze of horns and through a sea of people we headed for our next port, Latakia, a town on the Syrian coast, from where we hoped to embark on the final leg of our journey to Egypt and then onto Gaza.

Well may I remember that journey. A high speed, seemingly reckless and perhaps unnecessary dash through Syria at sometimes break neck speeds in what appeared to be absolute darkness, clinging onto life as we hung onto the brake lights of the vehicle in front, concerned that if we slowed down we'd be lost but concerned too that those following us might be left behind as our police escort with emergency lights flashing pushed us to our destination. More than once I thought we were heading off the road. More than once I felt the steering wheel go loose, losing traction as the road disappeared but finally exhausted from the concentration of the seemingly endless driving and not knowing if or when we would see our destination, we arrived.

Some people say it is better to travel than to arrive but on this occasion and under the circumstances it was the latter we were thankful for.

We had arrived, fittingly, in a camp which had been built in 1948 to house the Palestinians forced into exile during the Catastrophe, the Nakba, when 750,000 Palestinians fled Zionist murder gangs at the birth of the Israeli nation. This camp would again be filled with refugees as more expulsions followed Israel's pre-emptive Six Day War in 1967 and now again in 2010 when a band of displaced politicos and humanitarians would call Rumalla Philistine their home as they too waited to return to Palestine.

The camp was set on the shore line with the sea on one side and the town on the other. We had chalet type huts with between four and eight bunks beds. I bunked in with Tony and then Seamus and Joe from Tipperary joined us. A first aid station was set up, food brought in three times a day from outside caterers and there was a gradual settling down of the convoy.

We had been travelling virtually non-stop over the previous few weeks, each day a different destination and now finally we were at our last staging post before reaching the Holy Grail. The anticipation matched our high spirits; all we wanted to do was get permission from Egypt to enter Gaza. All the hard work had been done. We had travelled Western Europe and parts of the Middle East, this should be the easy bit, the last few hundred miles.

We had travelled in the full knowledge that we may have become ill on the journey, been involved in accidents and even faced untold dangers in Gaza, which was still systematically bombed from land, sea and air whenever the Israelis choose to do so. What none of us, who hadn't previously been on a convoy, would understand was the diplomatic web we were about to enter between Syrian -Egyptian relationships, between Egyptian -Israeli relationships, between Egyptian - Palestinian relationships and the fact that Mubarak was a Dictator not known for his love of Palestine. So we entered a political minefield and diplomatic limbo which would stretch our patience, our resources and our finances to the limit.

Now the reality which we had chosen to ignore during the road trip, as we focussed on getting to Syria, was upon us. The full weight of our own desires and expectations fell heavily on our shoulders.

Would the Egyptians let us in?

Would our efforts be denied, was it all in vain?

A journey of over 4,000 miles to show the Children of Jerusalem, the besieged inhabitants of Gaza that they were not alone, forgotten, or abandoned.

Would this message, our vehicles and medical supplies be left here like a discarded invitation, to gather dust and diminish with time?

The fear of failure hung over us. We all talked together and alone. We all wondered if our efforts had been in vain. My conclusion was we had already succeeded because we had tried. The awareness raised in Belfast, Ballycastle, Liverpool, London, Tipperary, Paris, Lyon, Milan, Ancona, Thessaloniki, Istanbul, Ankara, Damascus to name but a few of the places we traversed, along with the attendant media coverage, had firmly put the plight and fight of Palestine back into the public view and the public discourse. Yet I hadn't travelled all those miles putting myself at risk and willing to face what the Gazans faced every day, the risk of death or injury, just to fail now. None of us did. We had to get in, we just had to. Now began the waiting game.

For the first few days we felt like captives in the camp, unsure of when or if we would get permission to travel on so we began to organise the camp and ourselves. We arranged our own security to complement that of our hosts. We rostered double teams to record who entered and left our camp, a kind of roll call for our own convoy crew. We had the first aid station and cleaners for the showers and the toilets. I didn't leave the camp for the first three, possibly four days. We were constantly waiting to be given the word to prepare for departure. We had a convoy meeting each morning and were kept updated on the progress of the talks aimed at securing our arrival in El Arish, Egypt.

So a daily routine of sorts became established around security details, mealtimes and venturing out into the neighbouring streets where the Palestinian diaspora of '48 and '67 had now built their homes and their community.

Streets of houses built not from any official architect's vision but from necessity, one on top of the other overhanging the alleyways, a society born out of desperation but with much love. A community I sadly miss, as they were welcoming, friendly, hospitable and kind as many Palestinians are.

About a week into our enforced idleness there was a commotion. An awakening in the camp, a feeling something was happening. Then we saw it, a second convoy had arrived. Having believed we were alone, another humanitarian group made up of people from Qatar, Yemen, Kuwait and Lebanon had joined us having travelled their own marathon circuitous route. We watched these new additions in awe. All brand new vehicles dwarfing our own efforts. Doctors, professors, politicos, even a female airline pilot had joined us. So the West met the East and brothers and sisters conjoined in their efforts to bring aid, love and succour to a besieged people, a truly international effort with many religions and none.

If only we could all come together in enlightened comradeship the world would be a richer, safer place.

As the days passed slowly, we began to explore our host town more. What we wouldn't give for an internet café with Skype and the chance to talk our loved ones, to reassure them all was well and that we were safe.

I hadn't spoken or communicated with my partner Pauline since we entered Turkey maybe a week previously but we were in a small town in Syria. Where could we possibly find such a place?

Well it turned out there was an internet café across the street from our camp and several more just a short taxi ride away in the town centre. We were landed, happy days, time for ET or in this case Fra to phone home.

That elation when you first talk to someone you love from whom you've been parted for several weeks is hard to describe but I think we all know how it feels. Pauline was holding the fort at home running my business, while I was gallivanting around the Middle East and had probably been worrying every day. Now finally we could chat and via Skype which Seamus helped me set up, I could see her too. Both our faces lit up as she hadn't expected the call so her reaction was priceless. Pure joy and I felt it too. She told me my mum had phoned her every day to ask how I was doing and how proud of me she was. A typical Belfast mum or indeed mums anywhere, she didn't tell me she was proud of me but she told everyone else. You just gotta love your mum.

So job done! We were ticking the boxes. There were now over 150 vehicles and 340 convoy members. I had phoned home and started to eat out in downtown Latakia. I was witnessing the Syrian people, years before the Saudi financed terrorism would erupt, living in peace, harmony and safety. Soldiers patrolled the streets like police officers do in many countries adding to a sense of security.

I saw Christian women dressed like the women of Paris and Muslim sisters dressed according to their faith and I felt I was viewing life as it should be, tolerant, accepting and diverse.

Beautiful people with a ready smile.

It was also a time to really begin to engage with both my fellow convoyers and the Palestinians who lived in Latakia. After all, we can't claim to support Palestine and her sons and daughters under occupation and siege and forget the seven million who live in forced exile, many still holding the keys and deeds to their original homes in occupied historic Palestine, sometimes referred to as Israel.

And so as security relaxed at the camp we came and went freely as did many of the Palestinians living nearby. On several nights we held camp entertainment with songs, dance and music supplied by the convoy members.

Each day we had our camp updates, we had visiting dignitaries and finally we had the opportunity to repack ,reorganise and re-inspect the equipment, drugs and vehicles we were hopefully taking to Gaza.

As many donations had been given en route, like penicillin and other antibiotics, we spent several days checking dates on syringes, catheters, paracetamol, antibiotics, Ventolin inhalers, cancer drugs etc. First we sorted everything into groups, rechecked the dates of expiry, dumping anything that was out of date. One group had brought a portable x-ray machine, others had cancer life- saving drugs costing several thousands of pounds. We repackaged everything, having unloaded all the vehicles, itemised everything and taken an inventory stock. This would help us pass customs in Egypt and facilitate the hospitals in cataloguing our supplies. A very time consuming affair, one we had done previously in London and again in Europe. Personally I think the organisers were trying to keep us busy. Idle minds and idle hands are the playthings of the devil. If this was the case I resented it, doubling work for the sake of it never appealed to me. But it was done and a mountain of supplies left to bask in the Syrian sunshine.

It never rains in Syria in October we were told. The supplies had been stacked in the sun then overnight waiting to be replaced into the vans when the rain began.

I had been doing a midnight to four am security watch with John from Ballycastle. Our relief never showed up and being responsible and conscientious we stayed onto 8 am. When it started to rain there was Pandemonium. My first thought was "who made the decision to leave the supplies under an open sky when we had been under a marquee when repackaging everything out of the midday heat?" Some of the packaging was destroyed but disaster was averted due to the quick thinking and reaction of the convoy.

I suppose now is as good a time as any to introduce some of the characters and people with whom I became friends on the Viva Palestina 5 medical aid convoy to Gaza in the autumn of 2010.

Here they are in no particular order. From Belfast there was my companion Tony, from Ballycastle, Independent Councillor Paudy McShane and John. From Tipperary, Seamus and Joe, from Dungannon John Hurson and from Belfast Colin McShane and I will include our Irish comrade Mark from Liverpool who shared a vehicle with Colin. Mark was a true Scouser, down to earth, a member of Stop The War Coalition and a real gentleman. What you saw is what you got. We still meet up from time to time, I spent many an afternoon with Mark in Latakia and I consider him a good friend. We met up in Belfast on a few occasions and I mean to visit him in Liverpool. In London I first met many of those with whom we'd travel on the convoy. From Malaysia we had Azra Banu and her companions, a delegation of seven or eight. We had some fun following the Malaysians one time when we all got lost. I have travelled with Jemima on two convoys. There was the contingent from London, all mostly of Pakistan origin and British born with whom we got on really well as the Irish and the Pakistanis both know about British occupation and British racism. We were the Pakkies and the Paddies and along with guys from Birmingham and

Bradford we made up Charlie Company of the convoy. Then there are the Italian communists and socialists who joined us in Milan: a great bunch of guys and girls, very passionate and committed; a few Americans of whom I was very wary and one Canadian. This made up our merry band: the politically minded, motivated to stand up for Palestine, alongside the humanitarians, together with the brothers and sisters of Islam, all standing as one. We also had another Tony from London who drove the bus, Carole Swords with Ron McKay, George Galloway's close friend and political commissar, Nabil Hallak, a good friend to me and Kevin Ovendun one of the organisers who had been on the ill-fated Mavi Marmara. There was a father and son from New Zealand and Julie Webb Pullman and one or two others from Australia - all in all, a ragtag bunch of mixed religions, politics and idealists. If I've forgotten anyone please forgive me, I got to know some members of the convoy better than others. But together we were one.

It was the odd short conversation or that meeting of minds on a one to one individual basis that I remember most. That brief glimpse of the real person behind the convoy persona.

I'd like to think I got along with most people on the convoy. I don't remember having any issues with anyone that lasted more than a day or two although I had my reservations about one or two individuals who I suspected were more likely to be working for the intelligence services than for humanity.

I have beautiful memories of Latakia including one of the camp concerts. I'd actually been learning to play the guitar, not very professionally, before heading to Palestine and I had been making a terrible racket. It was a good guitar and had cost about two hundred pounds so I thought, if I bring it to Gaza, find a kid somewhere I would give it to him or her as a present. One of the New Zealanders had heard me playing in our chalet, then mentioned the camp concert and asked if I would sing a few songs Now I couldn't play anything from memory as I used music printed onto sheets with the chords above the lyrics but I told him he was welcome to use it so he played a few notes and I thought "Jesus, he's as bad as I am".

What I took to be my failure at the guitar was really to do with the strings being unplayable. All that way with a guitar, I thought I couldn't play and it turned out the strings needed changed. So off he went into town, bought a set of strings and hey presto, it sounded like new.

That day I'd spent the afternoon in town with Mark and headed back to the camp to find the concert already in full swing. The organisers had asked several members of the convoy to join in. The Haka had been performed by one of the New Zealand boys and his dad, with my guitar, was doing a few tunes .In the spirit of the occasion I agreed to sing two songs.

The first was one of my favourites which I sang as a tribute to my father Eric, now deceased. It is called *Arbour Hill* and was written in memory of Irish Republicans who died fighting the British in Ireland in a national War of Independence and whose graves are to be found in Arbour Hill Cemetery, Dublin. I introduced the song giving the brief outline as above and it was translated into Arabic so all those Syrians and Palestinians in attendance had an idea of what the song was about. Many of those attending had a workable knowledge of English.

I sang the song unaccompanied as I like singing and have a good voice, I know I carried it well so a second song was called for. Now I didn't want to sing too many rebel songs so I opted for the *Fields of Athenry*. Again the introduction to the song was translated. The lyrics were about a father imprisoned for stealing food from an English landlord to feed his family during the great Irish famine of 1847-1851. He was transported as a felon to Australia. Again, unaccompanied I began to sing. Now for any of you who are unaware the *Fields of Athenry* is an iconic Irish traditional song touching on the topics of incarceration, injustice, oppression, occupation and freedom and is beloved by many in Ireland and the larger diaspora. So when I began to sing my fellow Irish men and one Kevin Ovenden, convoy leader, took to the stage and before I knew it there were about six of us singing, very spontaneous, very poignant and very memorable. It was a camp concert to remember on a warm balmy evening with a microphone and PA system. Magical memories!

To sing a song about oppression to another people who had suffered oppression and were still suffering oppression under Zionist guns was surreal. We had a few camp concert nights but that's the one I remember.

Meanwhile, things were progressing slowly in our attempts to get to Egypt. George Galloway had arrived from London and along with a delegation from the convoy was heading to Damascus to meet the Egyptian Ambassador. They were taking some of the vehicles and holding a few press conferences.

I'd been invited on a day trip to Aleppo, the oldest market place in Syria, a beautiful Castle beside a walled indoor market. With Carole and several others we had an unforgettable day out. I bought Pauline a beautiful cashmere or silk scarf from the market.

That night we smoked Shisha and had a lovely meal in Latakia. We were joined by our Italian comrades, drank Syrian beer, told stories and shared bread.

Another night we went to a football ground where a select group from the convoy played a football match against a select group of locals.

Tony, Joe, Seamus and I visited a local school trying to make contacts to keep in touch with as we went forward. They turned the whole school out for our inspection and we gave a small speech.

Life in the camp continued but as time drifted by so did our thoughts of home and family. Now twelve days into our stay in Latakia I began to wonder how long I could leave Pauline holding the fort back home. If my money would hold out or if the ongoing lack of progress would conspire to send us all home and then the inevitable happened with over 340 people in a small confined camp. All it took was a wee bit of a tummy bug and down I went. There was no hot water in the showers but this was to be expected as the camp was used infrequently. So not eating, running a temperature, having frequent dashes to the toilet and cold showers made me one very sick and very sad young man.

I contemplated booking into a local hotel. Hot showers, clean sheets, a soft bed, a few medicinal drinks, it was so alluring and so tempting. I even knew the hotel to use and had checked out the prices. I decided that as I had been with my comrades on the convoy 24 hours a day for several weeks that leaving them for the creature comforts of a hotel would be a betrayal. So I shivered, had my cold showers, stayed away from people as much as possible and curled up in a wee ball until I felt better.

Finally word came through.

We were going to move, permission granted, we were good to go.

Rumours ran wild; one ship to carry our vehicles, our aid and ourselves; then the vehicles and aid would travel by ferry and the convoy members fly to El Arish; then a combination of both. Finally we were told a ferry had been chartered costing tens of thousands of pounds but it could only take 12 passengers alongside the crew.

Again the rumour mill swung into action. Would the boat be hijacked as had the Mavi Marmarra? Would those on board face summary execution as had the nine humanitarians on board that ship from the Israeli Navy under orders from the Israeli government?

I volunteered to go, not because I was brave nor reckless but because it was the right thing to do. Face the Israeli aggression and tell them we won't be denied the right to stand shoulder to shoulder with the Palestinian people. In the end I think everyone volunteered. There were over three hundred volunteers for twelve places.

We were warned not to stow away on the boat as had happened on a previous convoy. People's selfishness at times knows no bounds when they put others at risk to indulge their own egos. So, disappointed as I was, not to be guarding, shepherding our vehicles to Egypt, I was happy and proud that Tony got to represent us, the Irish on that boat. As for the rest of us, we were put onto buses, driven to Latakia Airport, put on chartered flights in relays and were bound for Egypt.

After weeks on the road and weeks in Latakia finally the prize was at hand, a fulfilment and culmination of all that preceded it. It had taken months to plan, months of preparation, a month on the road and finally we were nearly there.

A moment of reflection at the Grave of Furkan Dogan Mavi Mamara Shaheed (martyr)

The last leg

Chapter Four

Latakia, Syria. Former Palestine refugee camp.

We waited impatiently at Latakia Airport. I was in the second tranche of people to fly, so even though we arrived en masse at the airport many of had to wait for the first flight to load, take off for Egypt, refuel and return. As before it was a case of wait, then wait some more, then we were airborne.

Our arrival in El Arish had been well expected and well prepared for. We checked in through customs and I don't know why but I expected we would just walk through the terminal as ordinary arrivals get on buses and be on our way. What I hadn't expected was riot police in the foyer of the airport to greet us. Being from Belfast I'd seen how the police and army could treat people they viewed may pose a threat and initially I was struck by the air of menace. Batons were being waved around us. The point bluntly being made that the authorities would brook no nonsense. Bearing in mind we were a group of over 300 mostly middle aged, well-educated civilians, travelling on a mission of mercy with medical aid to Gaza I think the Egyptian government was over reacting to any perceived threat we might pose.

So as we all waited for the buses to take us to our accommodation the atmosphere grew less tense and more cordial. The buses had arrived and we had police on each bus and a police escort to a hotel by the sea. They wanted something like $50 per person with three sharing a room, a huge amount of money in Egypt and the Middle East in general, where many are paid only $1 or $2 a day. Added to that was the fact many convoyers had misgivings about supporting the Egyptian regime as many corrupt officials and army generals owned these hotels and so a standoff developed between those who were refusing to pay for the rooms with monies destined for Gaza and those who didn't want to upset the apple cart and wanted to play ball. I opted to join those in the revolt and in solidarity with them we held a sit down protest in the main reception area. It made quite a statement. Some of the convoy organisers argued against the protest and encouraged people not to be disruptive. Most of the objectors, myself included, then decided to end the protest but several hung on and refused to relent. To be honest I felt ashamed that I hadn't stuck it out but I didn't know the entirety of the situation and didn't want to have any complications between myself and the convoy organisers who had gotten us here thus far.

I was mindful that George Galloway and several convoy members had not been allowed into Egypt. Before we left Latakia George had called a press conference and the names of all those on the convoy who had been refused entry to Egypt were read out. They included a Sheik in his eighties and a young woman, Amena, from London. I felt there must have been a randomness to these arbitrary refusals of admittance as they made no sense but I was grateful I was allowed in.

As part of the agreement to enter Egypt and onto Gaza, George had been banned.

On a previous Viva Palestina convoy here in this very port of El Arish there had been a violent confrontation between the police and army on one side and the convoy members on the other. The convoy had been delayed at the harbour in El Arish, where some convoy members and police clashed as tempers over the delay flared. The convoy had been locked into a secure compound surrounded by Egyptian security personnel and subjected to a sustained barrage of stones and missiles thrown by the police and army causing several injuries that required hospitalisation. Those memories were fresh in the minds of the organisers and an air of mutual co-operation was being tried.

The hotel was beautiful and after a meal and a few beers I retired for the evening. I bunked in with Ron McKay, one of George Galloway's oldest aides and confidants and John Hurson from Dungannon Co. Tyrone, forty minutes from Belfast.

The following morning with the sun blazing in the sky we set off to complete the short journey to the port along with our riot police and police escort, to be reunited with our vehicles, our aid and our comrades who had travelled with them. How I would have loved to have been on that boat crossing. It was great to see our vehicles .It was the first time since we had bought the mini bus that I'd been separated from it. Tony and I checked the oil, the water and the equipment. With our passports in hand and with great excitement we formed the convoy into three lanes with our designated groups and call signs as we waited to leave the port. At the exit we would pass through there was a further police and army cordon and again an air of tension, a feeling anything could happen including violence.

I noticed some of the brothers from the convoy sharing water with some of the conscripts who appeared to be our guards for the journey to Rafah, the border crossing with Gaza. We waited for an hour or two, why I don't know, perhaps the security detail was clearing the road or they didn't want us travelling during peak hours. While leaving the port each vehicle was stopped and the passports verified by a senior military commander. I took the opportunity to shake his hand, while not endorsing the military dictatorship of Mubarak it was a chance to show we were sincere in our attempts to reach Gaza. We set off. The convoy was in good order, again with a police and military escort as we drove through the beautiful landscape of the Egyptian countryside .

I had been wearing a Palestinian Kieffa scarf from the start of this Odyssey. For some reason as we drove along I had taken it off. Somewhere, my intuition was telling me something. What that was I didn't know. As we passed a small house at the side of the road I noticed the family who owned it had come out to wave at us. A young boy ran down the hill towards our van. In a split second without considering my actions I cast the scarf in his direction. I looked in the mirror to see if the young boy had collected it. I couldn't tell. Later I was told by the driver of a vehicle following us that the military had stopped to see what I had thrown from the van. I just hope the young boy was given the scarf. To this day I am convinced the boy was meant to have that scarf, a souvenir of the convoy, a memory of the day we passed his home or an encouragement for him to garner an interest in Palestine. After all, we were so close to Gaza he might actually be from a family expelled from Palestine. Who knows?

After about forty minutes or perhaps an hour we arrived at Rafah. We parked our vehicles and entered the border crossing facility, a large building with seats offices a shop and cafe. Is it just military dictatorships or the Middle East in general but it took ages to be processed? Perhaps I was impatient to enter Gaza but the delays were very frustrating. They took our passports and we were left wondering where they went and what they did with them. Eventually, my name was called out. Passport returned. I re-joined the convoy and waited for the others to be cleared for entering Gaza. With engines running and Tony flying the flags of Ireland and Palestine proudly in tandem from the van, we crossed the border.

After a few hundred yards and elated to have finally arrived we disembarked from the vehicles to be greeted by hundreds of well-wishers, dignitaries, officials, charities and Gazans.

There were television cameras, radio mics, photographers, hugs and kisses. We were warmly embraced by the people. Some members of the convoy kissed the ground. It felt like we were a liberating army. The 300 Spartans! In reality we were 340 odd civilians who had travelled up to 4,000 miles to break the illegal Zionist siege of Gaza: young mothers without milk for their children, cancer patients without drugs and pain relief, hospitals short of electricity as fuel was rationed for the power station, building materials denied, an economy refused the opportunity to export goods, services and foods such as flowers and strawberries.

A crushing immoral imposition of a Draconian medieval type blockade of a civilian population of 1.8 million people, who had voted democratically to elect Hamas as their political representatives, a choice of which neither the Zionists in Israel nor the Neo-Conservatives in America approved: the staggering duplicity and hypocrisy of these states is at times breath taking. They demanded elections be held assuming their preferred partners in power would be Fatah but the people rejected Fatah and instead choose Hamas. The reaction of America and Israel was to refuse to accept the democratic will of the Palestinian electorate and impose a deadly siege in order to punish the people and force a regime change. A siege that continues today in 2017 to kill, choke and suffocate the economy, stifle growth, starve and at times murder the population and I haven't even begun to mention the military incursions, the aerial bombings, the shelling from the sea, the drone strikes, the tanks and terror of the Zionist army.

But for now I was content we had arrived, all uncertainty was gone. The minibus, the aid and our solidarity had arrived. After the press conference we had an unforgettable trip to Gaza City. It felt like the whole of Gaza was lining the roads to greet us. They had followed our journey every step of the way. With embedded journalists from Press TV in the convoy and Al Jazeera covering Viva Palestina in each country we travelled through I had no idea our arrival meant as much, if not more, to our hosts than it did to us. We arrived in Gaza City after dark. We followed our escort which appeared more of a cavalcade than a convoy and parked our vehicles near the government building in the heart of the city where we were again transferred to our accommodation. We parked beside a Ministerial building which had been totally destroyed by Israeli bombing and was now just a shell of a building a huge crater. We would be hosted by the Palestine Hotel on the Gaza strip beside the sea and adjacent to the port to which the Mavi Maramara and the sea convoy had been trying to sail.

Home at last, well it felt like home and would be for the next three days.

Our thoughts were with the people of Gaza, our family and friends at home and bearing in mind the Zionists had attacked the sea convoy bringing medical aid to Gaza we wondered what reception they might have in store for us. Gaza had been bombed several days earlier with many casualties.

Would the Israeli war machine leave Gaza unmolested during our visit fearing the international repercussions of murdering humanitarian aid bearers from many different nations in the world, including allies? Or would they send the international solidarity community, friends of Palestine and would-be siege breakers a message by targeting us? Well, we would just have to wait and see. But my view was that all those who braved the journey and crossed that border did so in the full knowledge that they could be injured or killed by Israeli aggression directed towards Palestine.

That makes them heroes in my book, soldiers of humanity, prepared to risk life and limb to do what was right and remind the world of the injustice of the siege and the right of Palestinians to self-determination.

We had interpreters with us at the hotel and on the buses. The food was brought in three times a day as in Latakia. Guided tours were arranged for us and it was an opportunity to walk freely around Gaza city and see life under the cosh. I had arrived in Gaza on October 21st. It was my birthday and I couldn't have asked for a better present. The hospitality we were shown throughout our stay will remain with me forever.

I think I took part of Palestine home with me.

Some of the highlights of our visit included meeting the families of the Palestinian prisoners, many held without trial in Zionist prisons under laws first enacted by Britain under the British Mandate, Administrative Detention, a form of imprisonment, internment without trial. Their stories were very reminiscent and pertinent to any nation-state that was occupied by Britain against its will, including India and Ireland to mention but two.

We met with the leader of Hamas at a civil ceremony and had the opportunity to hear him talk at Friday prayers. We were driven near the border to see the fields abandoned and unfurrowed as the Israelis shot at the farmers to prevent them working the land. We saw school buildings riddled with Israeli machine gun fire. We saw demolished bombed out houses, that hadn't been rebuilt or repaired because the siege prevented cement being delivered to Gaza. The people themselves took old, damaged plaster and rendered it for reuse. Several young men, many just teenagers, had been shot by the Israelis in an attempt to reclaim building materials from damaged houses in order to rebuild their own homes or sell to other house holders, a very dangerous pastime when Israeli troops are nearby, especially at the border.

Some guys even got the chance to visit the tunnels. I was given an invite but for at least one of those three days, I took to my bed feeling drained, exhausted and burnt out. All the travelling, the episode of sickness in Latakia, the waiting, the inherent danger of being a stranger in a strange land, the newness of everything, the culture shock of being out of my comfort zone perhaps or just a combination of all these things conspired together and I just kind of crashed for a day.

My other lasting memory is of a boat trip around Gaza port with Joe and Paudy, a tiny area more akin to a marina than a working port. Standing there one evening, gazing along the coast with the sound of diesel generators running in the background powering the hotels electricity, I saw the beautiful site of a brightly lit town or city just up the coast. With lights blazing it looked like a party for the eyes. When I enquired where it was I was informed it was in Israel, formerly Palestine, and many of the people living in Gaza as displaced refugees had property, homes and land there, now usurped by the Zionists.

The contrast could not have been starker.

The people ethnically cleansed from their homes, living as refugees driven from their own land, now under siege, living with food shortages, limited employment and financial disadvantage. Living in bombed out homes, with under resourced medical services, little or no hope and subsisting on UN subsidised education, food and work and those living with wealth and opportunities on a stolen peoples land.

What did they feel? What were their emotions? Looking upon this metropolis only a short distance away I would have imagined an overwhelming source of anger would engulf them. However, never once did I perceive anger, bitterness or hate from them towards the Zionist Israelis, just a deep seated desire for justice and a chance to live like human beings in their own land, with their own customs, beliefs and leaders, in peace and security. Surely after all they've been through it wasn't too much ask for, was it?

Three days was a very short time to try and view Gaza. The priority was to deliver the mini bus and the aid to the Al Awda hospital in downtown Gaza, so we collected the minibus and aid and drove to the hospital reception. We introduced ourselves and were greeted by some of the hospital administration. We were shown the as yet unfinished James Connolly Surgical suite. I chatted with one of the staff and confided that I was a qualified anaesthetic technician and was instantly offered a job. To have delivered the minibus and aid, to have completed what we started only ten weeks ago was surreal. We had done it!

The Irish delegation was invited to address a meeting of the Popular Front for the Liberation of Palestine. Tony presented the President with some hurling bats brought from Belfast as a gift set. I addressed the room and offered our unconditional support in their efforts to attain justice and freedom.

On the final night in Gaza they held a farewell concert with singing, dancing, music and entertainment. A few guys tried to get me up to dance a traditional Palestinian dance but I was too self-conscious. Within ten minutes they had several convoy members on their feet. It was fantastic to see everyone engaged together, a great celebration of our achievement, a fond farewell and an invitation to return.

A late night at the hotel was followed by early morning departures. We left again in buses with perhaps forty per bus. Back to the

Rafah border crossing and another long delay before boarding buses for the journey to Cairo. When we arrived at the departures area of Cairo International Airport we were separated from all the other departing passengers and corralled into a short corridor patrolled by armed police. We were refused the opportunity to go through duty-free which I could clearly see in front of me or a chance to grab food or drink from the nearby concession stands. Treating people who pose no threat like cattle does not help improve relationships going forward. Many of the convoy were clearly angry and an inevitable stand-off ensued. After a few hours things seem to settle down and I noticed one or two of the convoy had somehow managed to slip out onto the main concourse. I slowly approached the guard and slunk around him and went off like a rocket into duty-free to mingle with the other passengers. Then I spotted John Hurson, sure where else but at the bar. I joined him for a few beers feeling like an escaped prisoner on the run. My flight to Belfast via London wasn't until the next morning so I ended up sleeping in the corridor on a few airport seats.

We flew to London and I was seated with some of the Birmingham brothers. We chatted to pass the time. We arrived in London and before we could even disembark, Border Police, probably the intelligence services, took some of the convoy members off the plane. I thought 'here we go'. As I and the rest of the Irish boys passed through customs I was waiting to be questioned, but no, on we went. I ran rather ungraciously to the Belfast departure gate. There was only a short time before boarding and I was not sure how long it would take to traverse the distance between gates and terminals. At Belfast I bade farewell to the boys and grabbed a taxi home to Pauline. The sojourn over, I was just glad to be home.

With hindsight I could have engaged more with everyone on the convoy and all those we met. But I am glad we did it. I would not hesitate to do it again if given the opportunity.

From the River to the Sea, Palestine will be Free!

Entering Gaza, Oh joy of joys!

PART 2

Lebanon: The Summer of 2011

Chapter 5

Beirut Viva Palestina Summer Camp Lebanon 2011.
(L-R *Harry Reed, George Galloway, Ronnie Kasrils & Fra Hughes*)

In the summer of 2011, I attended the American University in Beirut located in a stunning setting with panoramic, sweeping views of the sea on the outskirts of the town, for the Viva Palestina summer camp - another creation by George Galloway's team.

I am not sure how I found out about the event, either online or perhaps the details were forwarded to me by another member of the Viva Palestina Convoy, quite possibly Carole Swords from London but either way, as soon as I saw that Viva Palestina were going to hold a summer camp on the political background of the

Palestinian Israeli conflict, I decided that I should go and made preparations to book my flights, sign up for the summer camp online and to arrange time off work and visit Beirut.

The event was extremely well organised. We left London and flew to Beirut Airport. We were met in the arrivals area and brought via shared taxi bus directly to register at the University for the Political Camp, then onto our hotel which was located a short five to ten minute walk away.

The summer camp was based on a series of talks with guest speakers. The topics would include raising awareness and consciousness around the plight of the Palestinians, the diaspora, the refugees and the ongoing injustices and military occupation of both Gaza and the West Bank.

I met many of the previous attendees on the 2010 convoy and Ghada Karmi, a Palestinian living in London and is a lecturer in one of the British Universities. I also met Leila Khaled who was involved in the hijacking of a plane many years earlier and an iconic figure in the resistance movement of the Palestine Liberation Organisation and a committed Palestinian revolutionary. It was a privilege to hear her speak and also a very proud moment to have gotten into conversation with her. I also met up again with Kevin Ovendun along with George Galloway and Rob Hoveman - all central characters in the running of the summer camp.

I also met Ronnie Kasrils, a white Jewish South African member of the ANC, the African National Congress, who had lived in exile in London for many years. When Nelson Mandela was released from Robben Island and went on to become the first black Prime Minister of South Africa with an African National Congress government, Ronnie Kasrils became the first security minister for the new administration so there was no-one more qualified to see the parallels between South African apartheid and the Israeli version being visited upon the Palestinian people.

Who better or more qualified than a white South African Jew calling for the democratic rights and recognition of the Palestinian people and indeed a separate Independent Palestinian state?

One of the many highlights for me of being in Lebanon was visiting the refugee camps of Sabra and Chatilla on the outskirts of Beirut. The camps had seen so much merciless slaughter of Palestinian refugees living there by pro-Zionist Christian Lebanese Phalange, supported and protected by the Israeli occupation of Beirut of that time.

I stood in silence with many others at the memorial statue in the camp as a mark of respect to those martyred. We were told the story of the massacre of which I already knew.

Another unforgettable memory is the day trip we went on to the mountains. We visited the Hezbollah Museum which shows how the fighters lived in the mountains, tunnelled out caves, storage spaces, sleeping areas, command and control stations - a huge undertaking, like the Viet Cong who defeated the might of America, who lived underground resisting foreign imperialist occupation.

Hezbollah tunnelled into the mountain side, manually carried anti-tank weapons and light arms up the mountains silently at night and engaged in a war of resistance against Zionist forces occupying Lebanon. A battle they won when Israel withdrew its forces in May 2000. According to the Los Angeles Times, 'this ended a military campaign of over 22 years against the Lebanese and Palestinian people'. The Israeli operations which began in 1978 included a full scale invasion in 1982 and resulted in the massacres in Beirut of that same year and ended with the illegal military occupation of Southern Lebanon. The Israelis left on May 24th 2000 under the cover of darkness.

I was invited to speak for a television recording to be played at the museum. I welcomed Hezbollah's victory and freedom for Lebanon and denounced continued Israeli military aggression within the region. I described Shiek Hassan Nasrallah as a true leader of his people and a hero of the resistance.

On our return from the museum, heading back to Beirut, we were afforded the opportunity and many thought the honour, of attending one of Sheik Nasrallah press conferences. As one of Israel's most feared opponents he addressed the assembled thousands during the live television broadcast from a secret location. Members of the convoy were given a special place from which to observe the spiritual leader of Hezbollah give his address. The night, the atmosphere and the words spoken weaved their magic for all who were able to listen. The night began with a play representing heroes of the resistance. It was very dramatic almost like a West End production of Les Miserables. Very professional!
The audience numbered several hundred perhaps even a few thousand and appeared to be held in a stadium or outdoor arena.
People were seated in sections. I saw the religious and various groups in different attire - some with Turkish Ottoman hats, others in full traditional regalia. It was something I have never seen before nor since. The silence as Nasrallah spoke was breath taking. His words translated to us were inspiring.

The camp held in July 2011 lasted four or five days and each evening in the hotel George Galloway would help lead the discussions based on the series of talks we had heard that day at the University or the day trips from which we had just returned. I even had the opportunity to go and have lunch with Ronnie Kasrils, George and a few others. These are opportunities I would never have realised had I not stepped out into the unknown, put my hands deep into my pockets and walked through the looking glass.

I met several people from the Viva Palestina 5 convoy and made many new friends including Jemima from Malaysia, Harry Reed from Scotland now living in Germany and still a Hibernian fan for his sins, Carole Swords, Nabil, Salma Yacoub of the UK Respect Party and many more.

Beirut is a beautiful city and its fractured politics where both indigenous and coloniser sit uneasily side by side reminded me of home. The weather was exceptional, the food healthy, the people welcoming. Having a beer or a meal out in temperate weather was good but what that summer camp did most of all was to rekindle my enthusiasm and passion for the cause.

I had self-funded my trip. One of perks of being successful in business is the ability to prioritize your time and your disposable income. These were treasured memories, never to be forgotten.

I returned home revitalised for the work ahead. Each step on the journey seemed to lead to the next. First the rally in Belfast in 2010, then the fundraising followed by the convoy, then the summer camp.

Now, what could I do on my return to Belfast to raise awareness?

Belfast BDS:
Boycott Disinvestment Sanction

Chapter 6

One of 70,000 flyers handed out at Belfast Castle Court Shopping Mall.

The BDS movement was spoken about quite a bit during the summer camp along with the one state / two state solution. Some argued in favour of just one state, call it Israel if necessary, as long as Palestinians had equal rights under the law as did the Israelis. Now on one level I agree with this, however, upon reflection I have concluded the one state solution encompassing coloniser and colonised does not work, democratically, governmentally, socially nor equally. To see one state solutions just look at North America, Canada, Australia and New Zealand to name but a few. Ask the Native American Tribes, the Innuits, the Aborigines or the Maoris if they have equal citizenship or equality under the law in their one state entities. I think we all know the answer to that which makes me in favour of a two state solution, where Israel and Palestine have a hard border but live in mutual peace and prosperity.

So BDS and how to apply it to Belfast?

There was a franchise in Castle Court shopping mall in Belfast selling Dead Sea products. I began a leaflet boycott campaign outside the entrance to the mall initially on my own before I was joined by Patrick, Johnny, Paul and Michael at various stages. My idea and vision was to begin this twice weekly boycott campaign at one of the entrances to the mall. My aim was not necessarily to remove them but to raise awareness around the issue of self-determination and nationhood for Palestine. In fact if I had succeeded in removing this group and its products I would only have had to find another avenue to raise awareness, perhaps boycotting McDonalds or Star Bucks who both have franchises in the illegal settlements or indeed Marks and Spencers whose company supports the illegal settlements in the West Bank and occupied Palestinian territories by donating tens of thousands of pounds to Israel.

So I had printed 1,000 A5 flyers demanding the closure of the franchise operating in Castle Court Mall selling products made from resources stolen from the Palestinian people and produced in the illegal settlements. There were usually two of us, me, Johnny or Patrick but at times we had four or five people to include

Michael and Paul. We handed out 500 flyers each Wednesday 12-1pm and 500 each Saturday 12-1pm. The total cost was £15 per week paid by those carrying out the boycott and we estimate we handed out over 70,000 flyers in the space of eighteen months.

That's a huge success in my book. It showed dedication, commitment and steadfastness. We suffered verbal abuse and the threat of implied violence from some loyalists and some fundamentalist pro-Zionist Christians. I learned on my feet how to counter their warped religious and political ideology. When I handed out the flyers I would make eye contact and say "support the people of Palestine, boycott the Dead Sea stall in Castle Court." I could usually tell who was going to barrack or harass us - they would put their hands behind their back so as not to accept the flyer then lean forward and say "sorry, what did you just say?" I would repeat my mantra "end the illegal occupation of Palestine, don't buy settler goods." They would then usually inform me that God gave Jews the land as promised to them in the Bible. I would retort that it wasn't his to give away then I'd ask "how old is the world?" Those who subscribe to the Bible as literally being the word of God will attest the world is 6,000 years old. I'd try to look incredulous and respond "6,000 years old? I've petrol in my car over a billion years old .Catch yourself on mate" .This usually ended the argument. Sometimes just being prepared to stand your ground was enough to put many off arguing, other times I would just shout over them, "keep walking, yeah that's it, keep walking mate, on your way" until they left.

There were a few occasions where some people squared up to us and we thought it might kick off but others usually stepped in and dragged the recalcitrant offender off. The flag protestors got lippy a few times but on the whole it was a worthwhile endeavour.

One thing I always wanted to do was to print a free weekly Palestine News update detailing house demolitions, settlement numbers, violence visited upon Palestinians, numbers in jail under administrative detention without trial, child prisoners, the effects of the siege on Gaza but I'm disappointed that to this day I have never managed it. I had thought the weekly flyer would be ideal for that but one week ran into the next and we just stuck with a kind of generic message. The ongoing injustices should be highlighted and nothing speaks louder than facts and figures but I guess the boycott campaign took up our available time.

After eighteen months the boycott work began to subside. People had work commitments; no new people joined us and so only a few of us kept it going. A few problems with the printers from time to time and a lack of enthusiasm from the public made our task just that little bit more arduous. We picked a number of around 70,000 and agreed when we reached it we would step aside. The franchise was still operating in Castle Court but more and more people began challenging them. They lied when asked where the products came from saying they were 'American'. We assumed those working at the franchise were Israeli and at times they had their own security watching over them. Those selling the Dead Sea cosmetics were all in their early twenties, both male and female, and appeared Middle Eastern. We concluded they were Israeli, probably ex IDF. Someone phoned immigration and reported them as illegally working here as Israelis do not have work permits in the United Kingdom. Two weeks later there was a complete change of staff but the franchise remained. On one occasion some local Republicans threw red paint around the kiosk symbolising the blood of murdered Palestinians. It was well received by many as Gaza was yet again being militarily mauled by Israel at the time. Some of the boycott team were questioned by the police.

Around this time I helped form Palestine Aid in Belfast, made up of some of the guys from the convoy, Paudy and Joe and my old friend Saeb who had planted the seed of my first trip to Gaza. We were joined by Patricia Campbell and although we were all well intentioned it never grew into the non-governmental organisation we had envisioned. It is very difficult getting a solidarity group up and running successfully and while Saeb and I tried our best along with Paudy, Joe and Patricia we struggled to keep it going. However, to our credit we financed three scholarships at the Islamic University Gaza; one in Law; one in Midwifery; and one in Counselling. We helped three students by paying for their tuition fees during their studies over the three year time span of the course. We also raised £10,000 to finance Solar Panels for the Al Amal children's orphanage in Gaza and made one off payments to several individuals to help alleviate suffering for people who had lost family members due to Israeli bombings and shootings.

While the boycott street awareness action has been paused Palestine Aid still continues to function as a volunteer non-salaried group seeking Charitable Status.

PALESTINE
Al Amal Orphanage Gaza Fundraiser
PALESTINE AID SOLAR PANEL APPEAL

CRUMLIN STAR

FRIDAY 15th AUG 9 till Late   DOOR TAX £3

Questions & Answers on Gaza with Dr Saeb Shaath & Fra Hughes 9- 9.30

Followed by music with **POL MACADAIM**

BOYCOTT Teeshirts £10 + Ballot on the night

Please support the children of Gaza. One of the orphan girls was murdered during the Israeli attacks and 5 were injured. Help the orphanage have its own electricity supply.
They will be taking in new orphans as a result of the war on Gaza.

To donate £3 please text gaza45 £3 to 70070

Find us on Facebook: Palestine Aid   Fra Hughes : 07425156263

One of many Fundraisers for Palestine Aid education projects in Gaza.

PART 3

The West Bank Tour

Chapter 7

In 2012 I had been in contact with Richard, a member of the Irish Palestine Solidarity Campaign who encouraged me to go to the occupied Palestinian Territories the West Bank. He advised me I could join with one of the groups that visit the Holy Land to observe life under Zionist occupation. Now I usually make my decisions pretty quickly on some matters but I hesitated over this as I had heard stories of activists being refused entry at Tel Aviv Airport, of strip searches and of deportations. I was aware of how those on board the freedom flotilla had been treated, some murdered at sea, all the others arrested and many beaten. So I had to check things out.

In the end I invited Pauline to join me and we booked flights from Belfast Via Manchester to Tel Aviv. We would be met at the airport and driven to Biet Sahour, a short walk from Bethlehem and occupied East Jerusalem. I booked the first night's accommodation in a hostel in East Jerusalem near the Damascus gate in order to avoid awkward questions on arrival. Our first taste of Zionist aggression came not in Israel via Zionist soldiers as I had anticipated but on the flight from Manchester. The arrogance of some on board was breath taking. Firstly, many ignored the steward's calls to be seated so we could depart on time - delaying us for over 40 minutes as if the attendants were beneath them.

Then during the flight we had many people gather for prayer at the back of the plane refusing Pauline space to walk by them to use the bathroom. I had brought a book onto the flight and a newspaper to while away the time. Both Pauline and I had agreed not to engage anyone in conversation on the plane mainly to avoid awkward questions such as, 'do you like Israel?' 'Do you support how we turned the dessert into an oasis?' I know I should play the game and act accordingly but I can't. I have to be honest and I was concerned I'd show my hand on the plane and be reported as an undesirable to the authorities upon arrival. In fact I kept myself so much to myself that I didn't pay any attention to the person who occupied the aisle seat beside me. About an hour into the flight I looked up casually to find three men talking and staring in my direction, I averted eye contact thinking it was strange. Shortly after, I looked up again and hey presto, the same thing was occurring. I wondered if they were trying to intimidate me. Were they air marshals or armed Israeli security personnel? I really wasn't sure what was happening. Then they came over hovering around our seats entering our personal space. After many minutes of this uncomfortable form of bullying, the man in the aisle seat brushed their hands off the head rests above us and I suddenly realised what was happening - this courageous, dignified young man who had stood up to them was Palestinian. I believe they thought we were traveling together and were trying to harass us. I would have loved to have chatted to that young man and explained how I had been to Gaza and was going to show solidarity and support for Palestinians living under occupation. I am sure he would have approved.

Alas, I stuck with the plan, said nothing and landed in Tel Aviv apprehensive about the customs check that awaited us. I knew what I had planned to say but in the end travelling as a couple, having pre-booked accommodation which we would not be staying in and prepared to give them the "we are here for a Christian experience of Jerusalem" spiel, I looked the customs border official in the eye, answered a few questions and we were allowed through. Never having been there before it's nearly impossible for them to know who you are or what your politics might be.

I had even gone as far a buying a British passport. In the North of Ireland we have dual nationality. Many pro-Irish like me apply for Irish passports and many pro-British acquire British passports.

Now, at the tender age of nearly 50 having my Irish passport stamped with entry visas to Syria, Lebanon and The Palestine Authority at Gaza, I applied for a British passport. The British are seen as more pro-Israeli in general and the Irish more pro-Palestinian and in my experience I've found that to be true.

Having arrived in Tel Aviv, Historic Palestine, with my virgin British passport containing only one entry visa stamp, we went to the taxi rank, met our driver and were whisked off into the darkness to Jerusalem. We arrived late and were shown to our room, advised what time breakfast was and made ourselves comfortable for the night.

The reality of our situation was that we had been in touch with a mutual contact in the West Bank who was able to add us to a group doing a two week tour. We would join them for the last nine days of their trip which included two rest days.

The following morning we had breakfast; tomatoes; egg; humus; bread; cheese; and olives, very refreshing and filling. We didn't really know the other guests staying at the guest house but before 9.30am with the bus arriving outside, we had met the tour organisers. We met the guy who had facilitated our arrival and we were now about to embark on one of our many day trips around the West Bank to include planting Olive Trees in the South Hebron Hills, visiting Jericho, East Jerusalem and meeting the Samaritans in Nablus.

We visited a farmers land in the South Hebron hills. It was a beautiful day and we were awe struck by the beauty of the landscape. It was one of the highlights included on the tour. If land goes fallow and uncultivated for three years, the Israelis say no-one is using that land so they take it- pure theft. The problem here is so many Palestinians who own the land were forced into exile and cannot till the land, so planting olive trees is used to secure the land for the next generation. On this particular day all those on the tour took part. We had actually joined a Dutch group who would be our companions for the next nine days. We dug holes in the warm sunshine, many of which had been pre-prepared for us. We met the farmer and his family and some Palestinian activists one of whom had red hair who I mistook for being Irish.

They made us a beautiful lunch and at one point a surreal moment occurred when some Israeli, American supplied, Apache attack helicopters flew a few hundred feet over our heads. It was like a scene out of Apocalypse Now. Flying low, I thought for a second they were going to attack us. They were frighteningly big, very aggressive looking and compared to the landscape of Palestine of rustic farm buildings and cultivated land, very alien. They flew on gaining altitude going God only knows where.

After lunch with the Palestinian farmer and his family we drove past a huge checkpoint sign saying it was unsafe or illegal for Jews to pass this point into Palestinian Authority Territory. It read like 'all Jews stop here, death lies beyond' It was really odd and discomforting.

Each evening on our return to the guest house we had dinner and Pauline and I would go for a short walk around Beit Sahour. Bethlehem was literally a five minute walk up the hill to Manger Square.

The next day our bus tour guide took us to East Jerusalem through the Israeli military check point where the soldiers boarded our bus and checked our passports before we arrived at what I can only describe as a cattle pen, where Palestinians who wished to enter East Jerusalem had to queue to pass through the Israeli illegal checkpoint. There was a priority channel for foreigners but we chose to wait in line with those who suffered this daily inconvenience. It was mid-morning and all those who had entered for work early had already passed through. Palestinians can sometimes wait for up to four hours in oppressive heat squashed together while waiting to enter East Jerusalem – yet another form of collective punishment making a simple twenty minute journey last several excruciating hours. When we arrived at Damascus gate we were met by a very tall, lithe, African looking gentleman. It transpired many Ethiopians settled in Jerusalem. Our guide was an ex-Prisoner and member of the Popular Front for the Liberation of Palestine. He brought us around East Jerusalem. I was shocked to see not only the amount of armed Israeli soldiers but armed Israeli settlers.

Both the army and the settlers were now illegally occupying this land. I saw anti-Palestinian graffiti, and viewed many Zionist Israeli flags on the roof tops and heard stories of how when one Zionist occupies or buys a house or apartment, they harass and intimidate their Palestinian neighbours out, then buy their property sometimes at a dramatically reduced price as no-one other than Zionists want to live beside other Zionists, all the while changing the ethnic balance with in East Jerusalem, a place which is meant to be the capital of Palestine but which the Israeli government now claim as their own.

Everywhere we saw the Israelification of East Jerusalem and the potential end of Palestinian hopes and dreams for a democratic homeland. We saw some streets similar to Hebron where Palestinians lived in streets that ran downhill while there were houses or apartments running up the hill. This allowed some properties to over-shadow the lower buildings. Rotten food, bottles, cans, masonry and human waste were at times thrown by settlers living above onto the Palestinians living below, necessitating the erection of wire mesh to be strung out above the lane ways so Palestinians could traverse safely beneath the occupiers above.

We saw how Israeli Zionists were taking over the markets; homes; businesses; livelihoods of the indigenous Jerusalemites; house demolitions in Silwan; and entry and work permits denied to Palestinians; the intrusions by Zionist into the Al Asqa mosque and attempts to have this most holy of Muslim prayer sites demolished for the building of the Jewish Temple Mount. Apartheid is how it's described and apartheid is what it is. After the tour we chatted with our new friend for about an hour having tea and discussing politics. He was well known in his local community but also by the Israeli occupation who seemed wary and ill at ease in his presence.

We then had a few hours in East Jerusalem where we walked the Villa Del Arosa., the Way Of Christ, to the point of his crucifixion at Calvary. The churches were ornate and the path well-trodden and although I have no time for the major organised religions, as a tourist I enjoyed the spectacle. The ever present armed Israeli soldiers always an intrusion I resented.

One aspect of Palestine I will always remember is the breath taking scenery, it truly is wonderful. It is worth visiting for the stunning landscape alone - the colours, the texture, the sky, it all paints a picture of what can only be described as deeply beautiful, indeed the Promised Land.

Next on the itinerary was Nablus. It is a Palestinian town in the mountains. It has a university and is home to historic soap factories and the Samaritan religious order. We were to visit all three.

First we went to see the university, a magnificent edifice overlooking a stunning gorge at the top of the mountain. I must confess it was the only time visiting Palestine that I felt some hope for the future. With Palestinians being corralled, their homes demolished, the Bedouin being systematically moved from their habitations like the Irish and Scottish land clearances. To see a modern well equipped functional university alive with the inquisitive minds of youth made my heart soar.

Our guide at the university was a young Chinese national who studied English at the University of Newcastle and now worked for the English department at Nablus University. He gave us a brief tour of the site then into Nablus town for a walking tour. Here we were then introduced to Kanaffe, a Palestinian dessert served straight off the pan, a delicious morsel, a very tasty and very welcome sugar boost.

Next we would meet the current religious leader of the Samaritans group which had its home in Nablus. We were brought to their Church on one of the highest points on Nablus with views stretching for miles over the mountains. Nearer my God to thee sprang to mind. The Patron of the Samaritans told us how they can trace their lineage back to the beginning of man. He told us of their incarceration under the Egyptians and how he personally can retrace his ancestry to the Biblical Adam as each Patron could. He showed us an example of their writing which he claimed was the first written language anywhere. In fact like many religions, he made a lot of extravagant claims. I pointed out the parallel I saw with Egyptian hieroglyphics but the point was wasted on him.

When he told us that the Samaritans and the Jews shared a similar history or perhaps a shared religious belief system and I recalled his re-telling of the incarceration story of enslavement of both people, I was struck by the parallels of some Egyptian religious mythology, practices and that of the Judaic Samaritan Christian orders, and wonder how much of Egyptian religious culture may have been assimilated into the Judaic Samaritan orthodoxy?

This is just a personal reflection based on what I heard that day.

Finally, late in the day we visited the world famous Soap Factories. What began as an uplifting heart-warming day of inspiration and hope came crashing back down to earth when we heard the story of the factories and of Nablus. Upon entering and leaving Nablus you cannot fail to notice the permanent security checkpoints similar to border controls established on the perimeter of the town, a population perhaps similar to Belfast, the permanent checkpoints, especially for those who' live under military occupation are a constant reminder that life can be ended, changed or crushed at any time, from summary execution during the intifadas, to arrest, to beatings, to harassment, to an inability of access to medical interventions during pregnancy, heart attacks and strokes. The power exerted by a foreign uncaring regime that has dehumanised the occupied, which in turn dehumanised the oppressor cannot and must not be under estimated.

At one of the factories we heard how the embargo on Palestinian products had caused catastrophic economic problems for the soap industry and wider society generally. How, during periods of unrest the factories had been subject to military raids with equipment being deliberately broken, summary arrests of workers saw a once thriving industry brought to its knees.

If you ever visit Palestine go to Nablus, you won't be disappointed.

Each busy day back in Beit Sahour was ended with the communal sharing of bread, an opportunity to reflect with others on the events of the day and to relax before an early night in bed. My one confession to make here is that as an ex-smoker I had begun the journey to become an occasional smoker. To be honest, it was a kind of self-medication, one or two cigarettes at the end of the day. It didn't encourage me to go and buy a pack the next day but it helped settle me down. There was always a palpable sense of unspoken violence. Anytime I was near the settlers or the Zionist army you couldn't help but feel that if you said or did something they didn't like, violence, threats and physical abuse would sometimes follow. It wasn't my imagination - perhaps having lived under oppressive military occupation I was more aware of the nuances than many. With over 700,000 illegal settlers, it was very unsettling, no pun intended.

We spent a day visiting a Palestinian Bedouin village near the J1 corridor. A new main road connecting Jerusalem to the settler outposts and further afield. There were Jewish only roads on which Palestinians could not travel. The number plates on the vehicle identified who was a foreign Jewish settler and who was the indigenous Palestinian native. More clear evidence of apartheid as if it was needed.

The encampment mainly consisted of several members of an extended family who had lived here and grazed sheep and goats on the land from time in memorial. It was only when an illegal settlement was established on the hill above the Bedouin camp that danger and death stalked the area. We were told how the local municipality refused to provide transport for the children to enable them to attend school. With no transport and the dangers of the busy newly built highway adjacent, the Bedouins told us how some of the children had been run over and killed by the settlers while traversing the highway. They were forced to keep their children from school so they built a sturdy shed to be used as a makeshift classroom. The municipality then demolished it and the villagers rebuilt it. A cat and mouse game between the occupied and the occupier began. We were also told how the settlers sometimes chased or shot at the children if they wandered too close to the settlement while herding their animals.

Pauline and I were both so touched we left a small donation. We were more generous than we thought as we had miscalculated the exchange rate and a small donation became a sizeable donation but on reflection we were there to support the people and what better way than to pay for transport to get them to the Courts in Jerusalem where they had lodged an appeal. We also visited a small derelict village, Dier Salem, outside Jerusalem, where every man, woman and child had been murdered by Zionist death gangs prior to the partition of Palestine.

Then it was on to Jericho and one of the rest days for the group before their departure. We travelled to the beach on the Dead Sea from where we could see Jordan across the waves. Little did I know that one year later I would be viewing this point from the other side in Aquaba, on the Jordanian West Bank border.

Pauline had on her swim suit, we reclined in the sand on a Palestinian beach. I am not sure whether the beaches are apartheid, Israeli and Palestinian, or it's just not safe for Palestinians to use beaches used by the settlers, but the beaches are de facto, separate. Considering the occupation and the settlers are illegal this is just another example of injustice where Palestinians cannot access their beaches, coupled with the illegal settlements which steal the resources of the Dead Sea on a daily basis to make their illegal cosmetic products, to make profit first and subsidise the settlements second, at the expense of Palestinians who have no homes, who are refugees with no jobs, hope or rights in their own land.

Pauline put on some Dead Sea mud, we had lunch and visited the Roman remains in Jericho, another reminder of a previous occupation.

These are just the highlights of our wonderful days, travelling round the occupied West Bank with our Dutch companions and Palestinian guides. Nine days in Beit Sahour, in great company with like-minded people, some religious, many not. On the last night we had a party in a local café bar. Some had alcohol, some had coffee, all had a good time. To our many friends on that tour I wish you well, great days in great company.

So we prepared to leave our hosts at the guest house and travel further afield. We had a few days left and had been advised to visit a few places on our own before we left.

Israel's security wall surrounding Aida Refugee camp Bethlehem in the occupied Palestinian territories. Writing 'Fra & Pauline, Belfast – Free Palestine!'

On our own

Chapter 8

To be included on that list was Ramallah, Hebron and the Friday protest at Nabi Saleh.

We walked to Bethlehem and took a shared taxi much like the Belfast black taxis concept to Ramallah where we had booked an apartment. The communal taxi dropped us off in down town Ramallah, an almost self-contained oasis in the ever shrinking geography of Palestine. We found a café and tried to locate our accommodation via Google maps but had difficulty with the app. Then yet another illustration of Palestinian, Arab and Muslim generosity manifested itself when many came to our aid. We were given simple, old fashioned, oral directions and soon thereafter we were outside our reserved apartment. It turned out the owner was a German who fell unsurprising in love with Ramallah.

Having found our apartment, we left our luggage and our first port of call was to be the Palestinian Prisoners Welfare Association in the West Bank called Addameer. I had followed their posts on Facebook and knew they had current, updated information on conditions inside the prisons. We set off with the address in hand, without a map and needing to continually ask those who spoke English to guide us. We stopped at an airline reservation shop in a small shopping mall. They reassured us we were not far from our destination and so we strolled further along the road.

We arrived at an intersection between two streets and saw a large imposing building on our left. We were on the right road near to our objective but there were no accompanying numbers on the buildings. I approached the entrance to one of the buildings and found it was locked but there was a side entrance with a security checkpoint. No-one was visible so we entered the building via a side door and went in search of someone to help us. We ascended one or two floors and found an occupied office. I asked for the prisoner's welfare office and was directed down the corridor. We politely knocked the door then entered. Three men were in a deep discussion and were unhappy we had disturbed their meeting. They redirected us to the Addameer offices which were situated across the street and they explained who they were. It was no wonder they were taken aback by our arrival, we'd stumbled into a meeting of the Palestinian Legislative Council in Ramallah. I am not sure who was the more surprised.

As we exited there were several armed guards to escort us off the premises and guide us across the road, they were friendly and approachable but I am convinced someone got a roasting for not being at their post!

A few minutes later we entered the Prisoner Association unannounced. No point in scheduling a meeting when we didn't know what time we would arrive in Ramallah. We were given a seat, coffee and tea and waited until someone was available to chat to us. My reason for visiting the Addameer office was to show solidarity with the prisoners and get an update as to how things were on the ground. To my surprise, although considering our links and parallel history perhaps I shouldn't have been, we were greeted by a fellow Irish man now working for Addameer. So the conversation flowed, as our politics were all the same and we found out just how difficult life can be inside Israeli jails not only for those incarcerated but also those who have lost their bread winner, the father, the son, the husband, the mother, the sister, the wife or the child to the Israeli war machine. There have been more than 750,000 Palestinians imprisoned by the illegal occupation since 1967. Many more than once, some for over 40 years some under emergency power legislation called

Administrative Detention - charged with no offence, having committed no indictable crime, not sentenced in the court but interned without trial or evidence for a period of 6 months which can be arbitrarily increased by another 6 months and another and another: similar to internment which was visited upon the Nationalist people of the North of Ireland in 1971.

Surely that kind of legislation has no place in modern democracies.

The Administrative Detention Act used by Israel in the occupied West Bank was first enacted by the British in Palestine under the British Mandated Palestine Laws after the First World War. From the occupied West Bank to the occupied 6 counties in the North of Ireland, British Imperialist rule needs no evidence to imprison those it occupies. Many Palestinians have gone on prolonged hunger strike forcing the Israeli regime to release them from this immoral form of detention. The prisoner goes on hunger strike, as Administrative Detention without trial or conviction means no sentence for the prisoner and no release date. Therefore the prisoner will have been kept, in a de facto prison limbo, expecting release after six months only to be re-detained as they prepare to leave causing hardship, heartbreak and depression for prisoner and family alike, prolonged enforced unending separation.

The prison regime normally forces the prisoner to enter the final days of a hunger strike and it is only when it's obvious they would rather die than to live in continued incarceration without charge or conviction that they are released. Israel fears an international backlash, a spotlight on its dark history of Palestinian imprisonment including some as young as 12 years of age for throwing stones. The age of criminal responsibility used against Palestinians is 12.

According to Addameer there are over 6,300 Palestinians held in Israeli jails as of April 2017, including; 300 child prisoners; 500 on Administrative Detention (internment without trial); 70 from historic Palestine now Israel; 330 from Gaza; 61 female prisoners; 480 are from East Jerusalem; and 13 are Palestinian Legislative Council members.

Many of the prisoners suffer life changing disabilities due to the severe nature of going on hunger strike and the devastating effects it has on the body including kidney damage, heart damage, and blindness. Many succumb to these conditions on release.

People have the right to resist an illegal foreign military occupation by any and all means they deem fit. Indeed the United Nations allows people under occupation the right to resist. It is enshrined in International law. I defend and support the just and legal resistance of the Palestinian people.

When Germany invaded France, the French resisted and formed the underground resistance groups in a prolonged war against the occupation. If Germany had won World War II and not Russia, would it be legitimate 10 years after the invasion to continue to resist militarily the military occupation? Would it be morally correct to do so? If it was right on the first day and circumstances had not changed then without doubt it would be right even 10 years on, or 20, 30, 40 or even 50 years as in Israel's illegal occupation of the West Bank and the Golan Heights.

We left the Addameer centre and returned to our lodgings having food on the way. Dinner in Ramallah was a Halal Kebab and then another early night. So much to think about, so much to process and tomorrow would be another long day

Ramallah was home for the last years of life for Yasser Arafat, leader of the PLO who was murdered by poison allegedly at the insistence of our old friend, Ariel Sharon, the Butcher of Lebanon and Israeli Prime minister. I visited the grave but Mr Arafat's body had been exhumed for tests that would confirm he was murdered with some form of radioactive poisoning: a very slow agonising death where he bled continuously.

He died in a French hospital in Clamart on November 11th 2004.

I had wanted to pay my respects at Mr Arafat's grave, just as I had at Furkan Dogan's grave in Turkey: two men who stood against Israeli aggression, both murdered by Israel, both unarmed and unthreatening to the state. I stood respectfully at his graveside for a minute's tribute and two guards took a photo for me as a memory of my visit. There are many views on Yasser Arafat and his legacy. To me he will always represent the face of the Palestine Liberation Organisation.

Having made my stop at the grave and monument to Arafat I got a taxi to take me to Nabi Saleh.

The weekly protest at Nabi Saleh, like many across the West bank, Bilin, Nilin ,Silwan etc, occurs after Friday midday prayer. This particular protest was against the building of an adjacent illegal settlement which has stolen most of the water from the village and blocked up their well. I arrived early, about 10am, unsure of the reliability of taxis on the Arabic weekend which is a Friday and Saturday. There were two other girls in the taxi and one of them asked me if I going to the protest and advised me were to get out.
I followed them as I didn't know where to go. I saw a garden belonging to a small village home on the corner with the main road. In that garden I saw several lines of metal wire strung across the lawn, I presumed for trailing plants to climb up. On examination, I discovered they were strung with CS gas grenades and percussion bombs that had been used by the IDF to quell resistance, peaceful and non-peaceful during the protests.

Welcome to Nabi Saleh.

The next thing I knew I was in the home of the Tamimi family[6], who had lost many close relatives to Israeli aggression both through imprisonment and death. I found myself having lunch and hearing first-hand how the village had been trying to defend itself against both settler incursions and IDF casual brutality. I am grateful at times when I realise I don't have to face these daily travesties of injustice. How the Palestinians find their dignity and strength in all of this creates a sense of inspiration and awe for me. I'm not sure if I would grow stronger or capitulate in the face of such overwhelming odds. Thankfully, I may never need to find out.

The protests and Israel's violent response is almost routinely choreographed. Firstly, Friday prayers are said in the Mosque, then people from the village men, women and children, reassert their right to protest against an illegal occupation which destroys their land, imprisons their people, steals their land and kills those who oppose it.

I am constantly reminded of how the Native Tribal Americans were treated by the European coloniser. Land clearances, outposts, settlements, bows and arrows against Winchester repeating rifles, reservations and land grabs, broken treaties and broken limbs. Israel is another European colonisation, this time of the Middle East using the template of modern America as it imposes its military and immoral superiority upon those it has conquered.

On this particular Friday I was waiting in the town square for the community to gather to oppose the occupation when I met two young men from England who were ISM volunteers. ISM is the organisation that supports people from outside Palestine travelling there for a number of weeks to record settler and IDF violence, including the destroying of olive trees and attacks upon the person

---

[6] Just as we were going to print, Ahed Tamimi aged 16 was arrested and imprisoned for slapping an Israeli soldier after her 14 year old cousin was shot point blank in the face by a rubber bullet. If convicted, she faces 10-14 years in an Israeli Prison

that are rife in the West Bank. After all, there is a daily war of attrition against the Palestinian people.

During the course of the conversation, I'd mentioned to them that I had heard that Miko Peled, son of an Israeli General, former Garrison commander in Gaza, would be giving a talk in Beit Sahour the following evening. To my surprise a voice with a strong American accent from behind me said "I'm Miko Peled" so after a short conversation with Miko everyone set off down the hill and the protest began.

The Israelis routinely raid and make arrests in the village. Some of the younger protestors, around 14-24 years of age wore scarfs to try to hide their faces but I was pretty sure the Israelis knew everyone in the village and would have had dossiers on all the residents.

Now the protest dance had begun.

The protestors walked down towards the Israeli soldiers who lined the road waiting to confront the peaceful protest. Then some rubble and boulders were strewn across the road to prevent the military jeeps from racing up the hill. At this stage I thought I'd seen everything in life when I witnessed what appeared to be the son of an Israeli general helping Palestinians fortify a road against the IDF. This was a somewhat Seminole moment. If only the world could see what I was witnessing. Powerful imagery! I Wish I had taken a picture. A few stones filled the air and a few CS gas canisters burned the skin, made our eyes water or made us choke, dependent on which way the breeze blew. I found myself standing in the garage forecourt. For any of you who have visited Nabi Saleh you will know it's at the top of the hill as you enter the village. A large projectile of some description landed right beside me, a bit unnerving as it could have really caused me some physical damage.

The disturbances were halted briefly as an ambulance tried to navigate through the village but was stuck at the road barrier created by Miko and the villagers. I ran down to try and remove the rubble to allow it to progress but was beaten back by the gas, however, one of the villagers got to the barricade and let the ambulance through. This cat and mouse game became more violent and more dangerous when the IDF decided it would occupy the village and so they moved up on the road and flanked the villagers.

Remember, it's their land and the occupation is illegal so they have every right to defend their homes but being outnumbered and the stones versus machine guns, Samson and Goliath parallels meant the young men from the village took to higher ground to continue the stone throwing , a futile gesture of defiance when the IDF were firing rubber coated steel bullets which could and did at times kill. The old and the very young retreated indoors and I found myself inside the garage once more trying to escape the skunk water the Israelis were firing. This is a form of waste water that has manure in it or something very similar, staining the clothes and leaving an overpowering vomit inducing smell of excrement.

One or two of those throwing stones in defiance to Israel's might were injured, some were chased and if caught, beaten and arrested. The protest ended and I waited for the next taxi passing by to return me to Ramallah.

I recently saw a documentary screened in Belfast recorded by two American film documentary makers that featured the Nabi Saleh Friday protest and in particular the Tamini family. It appears one of their daughters has become an icon of the popular resistance. She is perhaps 7 or 8 years old and videos the IDF attacks on the village, such a brave, dignified young girl. The torch of freedom with justice will never be extinguished in Palestine.

We had only stayed two nights in Ramallah as our time was limited and we had a lot to do plus we were familiar with Beit Sahour.

When I had left to visit the grave of Yasser Arafat before travelling onto the protest Pauline had been preparing to leave our accommodation and wait for me to return. She had been badly bitten the previous evening, Mosquitos just love Pauline and she was having a very bad reaction. The German gentleman who owned the accommodation insisted on getting Pauline ointment from a shop or emergency chemist and took her for breakfast, a kindness for which I will always be grateful. Pauline had her Thyroid removed a few years previously in an operation which went horrendously wrong, leaving her requiring a second emergency operation and a damaged Oesophagus which meant she suffered from gastric reflux acid causing her choking fits, a horrible thing for her to suffer and difficult in the extreme for me to watch.

I had travelled to Nabi Saleh alone as Pauline had already had a very bad episode of choking while in Jerusalem and I actually thought I might lose her so the thought of what tear gas could do to her was unimaginable.

When I met with Pauline it was five or maybe six in the evening.

I'd returned to Ramallah and knew exactly where to go as I'd walked Pauline there in the morning so we wouldn't be separated on my return. Pauline had arrived before the restaurant had opened but on hearing that I was attending the Nabi Saleh protest they insisted that Pauline wait for me inside and plied her with coffee and kindness, which I really appreciated. When I arrived, I ordered tea and we waited for a friend to join us. The world of politics is small, that of activism smaller and Palestinian activism even smaller again but Pauline and I were meeting up with a young woman, Razzan, that I had met at the Viva Palestina summer camp in Lebanon.

What a night! We met some of Razzan's friends and it was easy to forget these people were living under occupation. Good company, a few drinks and some Palestinian music left us in fine spirits. The next day we went to Hebron. We had been in the South Hebron hills planting olive trees on a farmer's land but this time we wanted to visit Sahudda Street, the Mosque and the market. We disembarked from the taxi and walked down through the market which was virtually abandoned. Only a few shops were open. We were browsing but not buying. We entered a leather goods shop and got into conversation with the woman there. She was part of a women's collective in Hebron were they made leather hand bags, belts, wrist bands and other products. We talked about the market and how the occupation was killing the local economy, the same story as in Nablus. It was the same all over the West Bank. A once vibrant market employing many, both at the market and in the community, supporting many families, was dying. We bought a leather handbag in a small gesture of support and headed to meet the Ecumenical Accompaniers who walk Palestinian children under 10 years of age to and from school past the illegal settlement and the IDF soldiers in Hebron who regularly abuse the children.

They took us to the roof top to overlook Shahudda Street, its Israeli military check points and the settlement. They told us of the provocation the children endure and how difficult it is for the Ecumenical Accompaniers to keep calm in the face of constant provocation as the children are provoked daily. Indeed one guy, an American, had been deported when he physically tried to intervene to prevent a young primary school pupil from being physically abused by a Zionist soldier. He changed his name by deed poll, to a legal but different name, obtained a new passport and returned. Clever man!

Then we entered the Mosque via an Israeli military check point. Now who in the world has to go through a military checkpoint to attend prayers? Hebron is a complete microcosm of the Israeli occupation of Palestine, the West Bank and Gaza.

There is a tiny illegal settler population that has been planted right in the heart of Hebron. It is heavily supported by the IDF and settlers, just like in Jerusalem, walk about heavily armed with automatic rifles. On Shahuda Street itself no Palestinian is allowed to walk along the footpath or road. Jews, settlers, Israelis and foreigners can walk along its length but not the indigenous population.

The Ibrahim Mosque is at the end of Shahuda Street and according to Al Jazeera was the scene of a violent massacre. When on February 25th 1994, a US born Israeli military physician walked into the mosque in Hebron heavily armed with a Galileo assault rifle during the holy month of Ramadan, when hundreds of Palestinian Muslims were crammed into the mosque for prayer. Baruch Goldstein who had immigrated to Israel in 1983 lived on the outskirts of Hebron. He opened fire on those at prayer stopping to reload at least once before being over powered by those under attack. Before he was stopped he had murdered 29 and injured hundreds of peaceful people attending worship. Many claim a second gunman was present in the mosque. Many other Palestinians were shot dead and wounded that day by Israeli soldiers when unarmed Palestinians protested outside the mosques and the hospitals treating the dead and wounded. The Israelis then ordered 520 businesses to close that night. They have never been allowed to reopen. The mosque was then divided and a synagogue built within its structure. Goldstein died while being restrained from trying to kill further worshippers at the mosque on that fateful day.

The Hebron economy, its market, its mosque and its people have never recovered. Devastated by all this brutality and trauma that had visited Hebron we returned to Beit Sahour.

Planting Olive Trees in the South Hebron Hills; under the watchful gaze of the illegal settlers their occupying army – the IDF.

The last few days

Chapter 9

Back at the guest house which now felt like our home in Palestine, where we had left our bags, we were in time for the talk by Miko Peled who was promoting his book *The General's Son: Journey of An Israeli in Palestine.*[7]

I am always wary of people who come from one side of a conflict and appear to support the other side. I always wonder 'are they spies or infiltrators trying to subvert the cause?' as has been proven in many conflicts all over the world. The hall was packed, the event very well attended. I bought one of Miko's books. I got a picture taken with him and the book signed. The thrust of the talk was based of his father's philosophy. We have Israel, let them, the Palestinians, have the West Bank and Gaza and live side by side in peace.

Makes sense to me!

Many Zionists want a greater Israel and that's what the illegal occupation of the West Bank and Golan Heights in Syria are all about. Indeed, many believe that is what the war on Iraq and Syria is all about. I hadn't realised until later that Miko's sister was in attendance and that her daughter was killed on a bus in Jerusalem by a Palestinian suicide bomber. That made me sit up and think. If she could forgive the people who killed her daughter then maybe

---

[7] Miko Peled and Alice Walker. *The General's Son: Journey of An Israeli in Palestine.* (Just World Books, 2013)

there was hope for the world. I would love to see her meet the family whose child killed themselves and her daughter on that bus.

What drives people to these extremes? For some it may be discredited religious ideology but for Palestinians I'd say it's desperation, a sense of retaliation for all they suffer under occupation. When you have lived under occupation all your life, it kills not only the human spirit, the physical body and the mind but also creates hopelessness in the soul, perhaps they feel all they have left to fight with is their bodies.

Our last day and night on Beit Sahour, such a short distance from Bethlehem and East Jerusalem, was to be our most memorable to date. It was January 6th, when Orthodox Christians celebrate the birth of Christ. We walked up the hill into Manger Square where we saw tight security around the Church of Bethlehem. There were crowd control barriers, lots of Palestinian Authority officials and armed police. There were people all over the Square, many celebrating Christmas day Orthodox style. Pauline and I stood at the police lines opposite the Square as the crowd gathered and the dignitaries arrived to be allowed into the church. To be honest I am not fan of the Palestinian Authority, I see that it enables the occupation and in many ways controls any resistance that might grow organically in opposition to the illegality of the military oppression. I had hoped to catch a glimpse of Mahmoud Abbas, the unelected leader of the Palestinian Authority, the West and Israel's favourite compliant Palestinian. As we stood in the cold, reminded of the rain and hail that had showered us earlier, we were surprised when after about two hours the gates separating us from the church were removed. I said to Pauline "hello, we might have a chance of getting into the church of the Nativity".

Sure enough, the first fifty people including us were ushered in. The dignitaries of church and state were already present in the most part and a small section near the front behind the Dias was kept for the common people. We filed in, wandered round and then took our allocated seats. What a sight! Three different Christian churches were celebrating the festival, each with a different language. Three simultaneous but separate masses were being performed. Incense filled the air, Psalms prayers of the faithful were sung and responses called out. Three times the different Patriarchs walked around the church preceded by men in religious costume thumping the ground with their staffs. I saw Abbas about 30 feet in front of me. The pageantry was glorious, the sight magnificent. I wondered how we managed to get here.

What a lucky opportunity or perhaps it was meant to be!

What are the chances of stumbling upon a mass with the whole Palestinian Leadership Secular, Christian and Muslim, all in attendance and getting in to witness it? Glory be, another cherished memory.

The next day we left East Jerusalem for Tel Aviv. Not because I wanted to visit the Zionist citadel but more as a counter for any difficult questions we may face on departure. My rationale was to portray ourselves as two tourists taking in Jerusalem and Tel Aviv. Why would solidarity activists spend money in the belly of the beast that is Tel Aviv? So we missed two days in Palestine but we missed nothing in Tel Aviv, not the nuances nor the racism we witnessed and overheard.

On arrival in the bus station we tried to get directions to the hostel we had chosen to stay in. We asked at the bus station. It should have been a short ten minute bus ride to our destination. At the bus station we were directed to a bus and boarded for our destination, we were charged something like €40 which I thought was very expensive. I repeated our destination to the driver and he assured us we were on the right bus. I had this nagging feeling something was wrong and the ticket price had confirmed it. Eventually, about ten or fifteen minutes into the journey I asked a fellow passenger who told us we were on the wrong bus. We stopped the bus and retraced our footsteps in the pouring rain, drenched to the skin and back to the bus station. No refund was forthcoming and I felt right there and then that some people in that society didn't really care for foreigners and non-believers. Arrogance, rudeness and dismissiveness were attitudes we encountered on many occasions from many different people in many different situations in Israel. Now I was not looking to find Israeli society as hostile or racist but that is what I encountered. It was not a self-fulfilling prophecy, I had no preconceived ideas about what I'd find but I now have no illusions as to how society functions there.

We found the hostel above a motor scooter shop in a side street. We had our own en suite room so all we needed was food, some alcohol and some breathing space. That first night we headed out around the district and were amazed to see how many empty premises were on view. You could almost feel the history of those streets, the empty houses a reminder of abandoned Palestinian homes, where thousands had fled for their lives to Jordan, the West Bank, Lebanon and Syria: the new Tel Aviv being built on the broken houses, broken bones, broken lives and broken dreams of the Indigenous population.

Many businesses proudly displayed the title 'est 1948' and I thought "yes, that's right, established in 1948 not 2,000 years ago but closer to seventy years." We found a small deli that sold New York style pastrami on rye. Although the food was necessary as we were hungry, we kept ourselves to ourselves. I had no inclination to fraternise with these interlopers and carpet baggers, many of whom were of military service age. Having had something to eat we bought a bottle of wine, some bread and crisps and wandered back to the hostel.

The hostel was home to those on vacation but also a motley crew of Zionist volunteers from America and Britain who appeared to be in Israel supporting the regime, getting subsidised accommodation and working in the nearby restaurants and farms. We settled down for the evening sitting near to but separate from the others. I advised Pauline not to talk but just to listen. There was a young Canadian girl who one of the resident hostel workers was trying to bait. I heard him tell her how the Jews had the made the desert bloom, how it was our duty to protect Jews against anti-Semitism and defend Israel. As someone outside of the conversation it was apparent he was trying to get her to agree or disagree with his opinion and suss her out. It felt almost like bullying. Eventually after about an hour of this the girl, evidently in distress and in agitation said "why would you assume I am pro-Israeli just because I am Canadian?" Bingo! He had her and we all knew her politics. So I looked around and wondered how many other pro-Palestinians were disguising their feelings like me and Pauline. We headed to bed only to be kept awake half the night by the Zionist English staff, talking loudly, laughing and drinking in the communal area outside our room. I will never forget how shortly after the Canadian headed to bed the young man who had been goading her said to his companions "see? I told you she was against us."

A nice lesson in the art of keeping quiet while observing what was happening around you.

We had briefly spoken to one or two people staying at the hostel that night when we were on the balcony having a smoke. One confided in us that he was from the Ukraine, there to visit his son. I think he guessed our thoughts but we just talked politely and said very little. The next day I wanted to go Nazareth, a small village or town in the country side.

We went to the bus station to get tickets and information. This is where we found there are either two places called Nazareth or the bus only went to the Jewish community and we had to get a taxi to our final destination. We had contacted a human rights organisation there and we were hoping to visit. When the woman at the enquiries desk heard our destination was the Arab

Palestinian town village of Nazareth, again either she was rude through pure ignorance or she didn't want to help us.

I was a bit lost in a strange, unfriendly city so Pauline and I were not sure if we used public transport if we could get there and back in one afternoon as we had an early flight the next day. The woman was disdainful when asked for her help. In the end, I made a decision I subsequently regretted. We gave up on our trip to Nazareth and headed down the port of Haifa. I learned on my return to Ireland that had we gone to Nazareth we would have met one of the Palestinians elected to Israeli Knesset, Haneen Zoabi. It's a small world. Haneen had stayed at our guest house in Belfast the year before. What a pleasant surprise it would have been for both of us to get reacquainted. Moreover it would have confirmed her belief in Irish solidarity activists to have met me in Belfast and then again in Historic Palestine.

We found the main beach beside the port and I was astounded to hear the call to prayer from a mosque. I spotted the minaret and we ascended above the port to see the Mosque located near to a Christian church. We walked along the beach and went in search of a Shisha bar. We saw a café where men were playing cards outside and Shisha pipes in the doorway. While we were deliberating taking a seat I was approached by a guy who said "come here my friend, come here look at our beautiful place, clean and nice, don't go there it's dirty." So we were talked into having Sisha in a nearby bar where he had tobacco tablets and not the resin which was on offer at the café. With hindsight, I think we were led away from a Palestinian café into an Israeli bar.

Again in the evening we went for food. A little café bar restaurant. The food was very expensive for all we had and again we kept pleasantries to a minimum, avoided the other guests and ate in quiet contemplation. I asked for the bill and paid the waitress. Now I paid the entirety of the bill but didn't leave a tip. The waitress went ballistic and demanded a tip as if it was an entitlement and refused to accept payment of the bill. I stood my ground refusing to be blackmailed into paying a tip in a society built on genocide. I bought food because it was it was a necessity, alcohol because Pauline and I wanted to chill out over a glass of wine. I had paid the hostel and the buses and the train but I wouldn't pay one more penny than I had to in an Apartheid racist country. I eventually walked to the bar, left the bill and the payment and presumed the waitress was somewhere sticking needles in a doll that was made in my image.

Later that night we reflected on the day we had, quietly in our room. The dismissive attitude of the woman in the bus station; the rude waitress; the homeless black people living in tents subject to racist taunts and attacks; black Jews who travelled from Ethiopia and the African subcontinent to Israel to be treated as racial inferiors by some. It is unbelievable that Jews and Zionists can be anti-Semitic when it comes to colour.

That last night was a carbon copy of the night before.

The young English Zionists smoking and drinking. Pauline and I were on our phone on Facebook, logging out after each session lest the phones be examined on departure. I had not taken any pictures of anyone we met, only scenery, our pictures of me and Pauline in Jerusalem, Jericho and Tel Aviv.

There was an American guy, tall, young, early twenties. He was talking to someone when we went onto the smoking terrace. We got a light for our cigarettes and he was saying how he couldn't wait to join the Israeli Army. Now I thought this was surreal. He was full of hate for the Palestinians and couldn't wait to serve in the occupied territories of the West Bank. I thought "holy Jesus, this guy wants to beat and kill Palestinians, show them who's boss and claim more land for the greater Israel project." I said, "Excuse me, I'm confused. Aren't you American? Should you not be defending America? Can you even join the Israeli army?" He explained that he had to be resident for six months and then he could join. I asked about America. His reply was "fuck America, I'm for Israel." There and then I decided Palestine was in far more jeopardy than I had previously realised. This guy was a header, he was going to kill people.

The next day we walked to the train station to board our train to the airport. We could have taken a bus but I preferred to walk. We were assured it wasn't far. I stopped a shop keeper to check our direction but he just waved us away like we were an irritating bumble bee.

Boy, was I glad to heading home?

All that time in the occupied West Bank and people were so kind and friendly and no hatred spoken off towards Israel. Two days in Israel and I was so happy to get out.

We checked in at the airport and were put on a bus to take us to a distant departure gate. Anyone who was Jewish boarding our flight was ushered through customs like regulars at a night club. There literally was a rope and hook that was lifted to allow progress yet non-Jews, about twenty five of us on the Manchester flight, were brought through a security check. They seemed to assign a border guard to each individual or couple flying. He took our passport, invited us forward and put both us and our luggage through some checks. He asked us when we had arrived, if we had made any friends in Israel and why we had visited? - All fairly innocuous questions but each with a destination in mind. He obviously wanted to suss us out but not to too aggressively.

I assured him we had been on a pilgrimage of sorts and hadn't left Jerusalem except to the beaches of Tel Aviv, the cover story was coming in handy after all. Then as part of this gentle yet invasive interrogation he asked "where did you buy that handbag?"
I answered "Jerusalem."

Pauline was wearing the bag we had bought on our solidarity visit to Hebron and I instinctively felt that was what he was suggesting. Pauline's cigarettes had been bought in Bethlehem, they were Palestinian and we bought two hundred of them to take home. I loved their name. They were called 'Victory'.

They proceeded to scan our luggage. That was when I was grateful I had resisted the urge to bring along a spent gas grenade that resembled a hand grenade I had seen in the guest house. I thought if they had discovered that and said it was IDF property or accused me of rioting I would be in trouble. I felt I answered all his questions smoothly and not too defensively. I'd made a comment to Pauline for his benefit about how unusual it was to get the third degree, sure for goodness sake we were only there on holiday. When the questioning stopped he decided a physical search of our bags was in order so our luggage was brought to another table in front of the other departing passengers. The woman searching our bags was obviously at a loss as to what she should be looking for. She glanced over at the guy who had asked for the search perplexed but he just shook his shoulders and watched on. I was just hoping all the time that she wouldn't find the two small plastic bullets about the size of a lozenge which the Israeli military fire at the Friday protests that were secreted in my socks in my luggage bag. A souvenir from Nabi Saleh!

All that effort, all those little mistruths could be about to be undone and I would be banned from visiting Israel and the West Bank potentially for up to ten years. Well, panic over! She never found them. Thankfully they are quite small.

However, a young Muslim man was having his bags searched too but what a contrast. The same woman who gave my bags a cursory look, took out this young man presents, underwear, clothes and shoes, put them out on public view as other passengers looked on, looked them up and down as if they were contaminated and made him stand in full view of everyone else in the departure lounge. The message was loud and clear, Muslims with beards are the people to be frightened of! If he had been Jewish and these were fascists conducting the search, there would be a righteous and deserved outcry but the searchers were Jews and the victim Muslim. History repeating itself with a twist, this time Jews weren't the victims of fascism, they were the perpetrators.

We boarded the flight and headed for Manchester.

On arrival we waited at the carousel with one or two of those who had been on our flight over and who still seemed interested in Pauline and me, as if trying to figure out why we had gone. I approached the young Muslim brother, told him I'd been to Gaza with some of the brothers from Birmingham and I wished him well. On leaving the carousel I felt compelled to say something. Witnessing the many things we had on our 14 day visit I shouted, "From the river to the sea, Palestine will be free." I walked past two airport security personnel half expecting to be pulled in but went out into the airport concourse to find details of our flight to Belfast.

Part 4

Gaza: The Solo Run

Chapter 10

Egyptian Father who attended Tahrir Square, Cairo, every day with a photo of his murdered son.

Still heavily involved in the struggle to raise awareness and show solidarity for the right of Palestinian self-determination and an end to the illegal occupation of the West Bank and lifting the siege on Gaza, I was still in loose infrequent contact with some of the people I had met in Gaza and I was also developing an electronic relationship with the Islamic University in Gaza (IUG) where we had hoped to sponsor one or more scholarships. In the end we financed three scholarships over three successive years of which I'm quite proud.

We had a problem with the bank transferring the money. We had tried on several occasions, one time the monies had left our Palestine Aid account but was refused or returned by the recipient bank. I must say, I have now discovered how simple international bank transfers are but the counter staff at my local bank hadn't a clue. Perhaps if they had been more efficient, experienced or on the ball I might have saved myself a trip.

As it turned out I decided to combine two desires in one trip. I wanted to take Pauline on holiday, as we did every year just after Christmas or the New Year holidays, as the guest house was closed and we had no bookings. I thought we would go somewhere the sun is shining, where we can get some heat into our bodies, long days by the pool or beach, some nice food and drink and it would shorten our dark, cold, Irish winter. By now I had raised over £3,000 for the scholarship at IUG and was keen to get the monies there. I had spoken to a few friends in Gaza who told me that the border was open at Rafah and access was available. I had heard previously that access to Gaza was restricted and foreigners needed to apply in advance so I questioned my contacts who assured me there were no problems. So an idea began to formulate in my mind.

What if Pauline and I booked a two week holiday in Sharm el Sheik thus taking care of our holiday arrangements for that year? I went to Thomas Cook travel agents in Belfast and saw a two week all-inclusive beach and hotel package which suited us perfectly. Then I suggested to Pauline that I go a week or ten days earlier and visit Gaza before meeting her in Sharm el Sheik. Would she be ok traveling alone? Would it be ok if I went as planned? I have to give Pauline her dues, she has always supported my activism and she once confided "I know you Fra, if I said no you'd do it anyway." She's right, I ask her permission but I'm determined to go. What's the old saying? 'Better to ask for forgiveness than seek permission.'

Plans made, passport in hand, flights booked from Dublin to Cairo with an overnight in a hotel near the airport, then off to Gaza by bus. Everything was going to plan, on time and on schedule. I arrived in Cairo, took a taxi to my hotel at an agreed price of $10 then went out for a short tour of the local streets. Many people would have made more of their time there but to be honest, I'm not the tallest, most physical specimen on the planet so being on my own I just strolled to the shops and back to the hotel. After an early breakfast I took a taxi to the local Al Masri bus station. The taxi journey was far longer than the one from the airport but much cheaper. Airport taxi drivers are the same all over the world; some of them are rip off merchants.

I was struggling at the bus station as to my destination. I was going to Gaza via Rafah but they kept saying El Arish. Eventually someone came to my assistance and explained that I had to go to El Arish first before I can make my way to Gaza. I gave this good Samaritan an Irish key ring as I'd brought gifts and souvenirs from Belfast to leave in Gaza. In return he handed me some scented oil for my skin to soothe any bites or sunburn I might get. I explained that I was Irish and was going to Gaza to support the Palestinians. He shook my hand and wished me well.

The journey would be around 6 to 8 hours and the coach pulled out of the bus station to merge with the traffic. The bus was pretty full as we set off. I, as usual, just kept to myself not sure who to confide in or if the language barrier would prove difficult and after a few hours the bus pulled into a terminal. It became apparent after everyone exited that this bus wasn't going any further. I panicked thinking I must have gotten on the wrong bus but this was a simply change over stop and I had time for tea and sandwiches before we boarded a different bus to continue our journey. To pass time on the road I just looked out the window and wondered what I would do in Gaza. I had nothing planned except to go to the university and hopefully meet the student and his family, pay the scholarship, conduct a video and interview on behalf of Palestine Aid, record some stories of life under siege and the destruction wrought by Israeli aggression.

We crossed the Suez Canal and I took a few photos.

There was a combined security check at the bridge over the Canal: a stop off point to allow people to have lunch and use the facilities. I must say it was very civilised, off the coach into a cool air conditioned mall and restaurant. The Suez Canal appears to have a permanent military check point. I suppose it is a vital piece of Egyptian infrastructure and would be one of the first places attacked in any renewed hostilities with Israel. The bus was boarded at the check point and identity papers checked. I surmised that as I was a foreigner it brought me to the attention of the guards, they briefly looked at my passport and took everyone off the bus. We had to locate our bags from the luggage trunk and put them in front of us. Sniffer dogs then checked out our bags, all was in order so we were allowed to proceed. While waiting to re-board the bus I was approached by a middle aged man smoking a cigarette. He casually inquired where I was going to which I replied "El Arish" after all, that was the destination of the bus. He then asked me where I was going after that and I told him "Gaza". He showed me his Palestinian Passport and said he was going home and suggested we could share a taxi to the border crossing. I'd heard of this happening before and decided to accept his offer.

Before we reached our destination there was a university outside El Arish. The bus stopped and the stranger beckoned to me to disembark. Now this was a surprise! I thought we were going to the bus station and I could see one or two people on the coach wonder why I, a stranger at the back of the bus, was getting off with a guy at the front of the bus, so my antenna began to twitch. I had been watching this man from time to time and I had seen him on his mobile phone. We got off the bus and hailed an ancient Mercedes taxi which I thought had been following the bus because he didn't drive around the bus as you would expect when it stopped. This kind gentleman who had offered me a lift then said to me, "Don't speak while you are in the car, I will do the talking."

Things were becoming a bit nervy; the phone calls prior to exiting the bus; the taxi that appeared to be waiting for us; and combined with the command not to speak as I sat demurely in the back seat made me question my decision to travel with him. My new found friend was chatting away in Arabic, I could see the driver looking at me in the rear view mirror during their conversation and I saw my companion now had two cell phones and was alternating between them. The driver must have been travelling at 80 miles per hour. I suddenly thought of 'plausible deniability'. That's where if they ever question the driver about my being in the car he could honestly say "I've no idea who the second passenger was, he never spoke a word." For a split second I thought of Brian Keenan, the Belfast man kidnapped in Beirut. He was badly beaten from time to time, chained to a radiator and not released for four and a half years. I had a mental picture of being hooded and forced into captivity. These were my thoughts for about twenty minutes in the car before I saw a sign for Rafah, the same sign I'd seen on the convoy. Happy days, we were definitely on the road to the border crossing. Relief flooded through me. I had taken a gamble and it was ok, it turned out he was a man of good character. Those two phones really worried me so I asked him about them. He explained that one was local for Gaza and the other had a different SIM card for Egypt: perfectly understandable when you hear the rationale behind the need to have two phones.

Not for the first time on my journeys my need for assistance resulted in my reaching out to strangers for help, support and friendship without which I would have been truly lost and insecure. This was fantastic, in about an hour I'd be through the border and in the company of friends in Gaza. Wouldn't I?

We walked together to the entry gate at the border crossing. This Palestinian who had been visiting friends and family in Egypt refused to accept any payment towards the taxi fare. He advised me that if there was any trouble getting in, I should go back to Cairo. I thanked him for his help and advice and we parted. I gave my passport to a border guard who smiled and said he would return shortly. Approximately 30 minutes later he came back. He asked me if I had paperwork or a visa to enter Gaza. I explained that I had a tourist visa for up to three months which allowed me travel freely throughout Egypt but I now realised the restrictions affecting foreigners were still in place. I had been misinformed! I had taken other people's enthusiasm for my visit as fact. I had believed them when they said "Fra, come, the border is open. We will wait to greet you."

I had hoped to be met by a journalist friend Yousef al Helou who resided in Gaza. Now I realised I was unprepared for what I'd undertaken. I had only my UK mobile and wasn't sure how to contact Yousef. I had not bought a prepaid mobile phone bundle to allow calls in the Middle East as I had chosen to use Wi-Fi where ever it was available. So now at four o'clock in the afternoon I found myself stranded at the point of entry to Gaza. I now faced a dilemma. What would I do now?

There was a young Egyptian lad who had been hovering about me for a while. I wasn't sure what he wanted. He began gesturing to me with his hands to make himself understood. He was moving his hand down and under in a fluid movement, I suddenly realised what he meant when he accompanied the gesture with the phrase $50. That was the price of the tunnels. That was what he was saying, "come with me, $50 through the tunnels." I had travelled all the way to Gaza expecting to be allowed to enter. Now I was considering walking off into the desert with a complete stranger .I had to admit, I had been spooked by the taxi ride and it was one of those split second decisions, take a chance to get in, put your safety at risk with this young man or take time to review your options. I said "thank you, but No."

Perhaps this was a mistake in hindsight but we will never know. As I pondered my position another young man with a pony tail approached. He asked me if I would meet his father a few feet away at a café beside the border post. The first thing that struck me was that he didn't look very much like his dad and had a different accent. The boy was white; the father looked Middle Eastern; and had the worst Texas accent I have ever heard. I felt the picture didn't ring true.

We chatted about where I was going in Gaza. He enquired if I was part of a delegation. Then he said, "Stay with us, wait until the border post is closed, pay $300 and the guard simply walks you through or around the border post. I had two immediate concerns. Firstly, I hadn't travelled to Egypt to encourage greed and corruption and secondly I thought "what if $300 gets you in but you need to pay to get out? Did this price include the outward journey and would I get the passport signed officially?" I should have asked these questions but my mind was full of only one question, "What do I do?" The border was beginning to close. All those associated with border business, the café, taxis, porters, had all began to drift away. I had no experience nor had I been given any advice as to a plan B if I was refused entry. I decided I hadn't really travelled just to bribe my way in and in the circumstances so as an Irish traveller I decided to contact the Irish embassy in Cairo for assistance.

I got in the last taxi leaving the border, a big Mercedes carrying 8 people, about 40 years old and I began the long journey back to Cairo. I had agreed a price with the driver and we stopped once on the way back for 30 minutes for food and to use the facilities. I was beginning to panic. I was heading to Cairo arriving around midnight to one am with no accommodation. Would I be walking the streets aimlessly at the mercy of local society? Would my body be found up an entry, robbed and with my throat slit? I'd like to think these are rational fears for a lone traveller in a foreign country, unable to speak the language, carrying money, passport and cameras. Perhaps it was just a combination of factors which had started with the earlier taxi ride.

So here we were. The driver dropped all the other passengers off at a roundabout and asked where I wanted to go, I could only be truthful, I said "I do not have anywhere to stay." He asked if I trusted his judgement and I said I did. In reality, I had no other choice. He took me to a good hotel, a bit more expensive than I would have liked but I was grateful to him. With a room reserved I headed to my bed for a sleepless night after an exhausting day, both physically, mentally and emotionally.

I got up early the next morning and had another light breakfast, eggs and breads with coffee, and went to reception to use the Wi-Fi. "Sorry, we do not have the Internet" came the reply. I was pretty shocked as it was a good hotel. I was advised there was an internet café around the corner. I walked to the café to find a sign in the window with a clock a showing a time which I presumed meant it opened at 4pm. It was 10am and all I had wanted was the address of the Irish embassy. A simple Google search would have taken all of ten seconds. So day three was spent in Cairo when it should have been day one in Gaza. What should I do now? I had Egyptian pounds in my pocket and an embassy to visit.

I hailed a taxi and asked the driver in English if he knew the way to the Irish embassy. I assumed the taxi drivers would have an idea of its location but unfortunately it was a destination never previously requested. After some confusion and a few minutes silence I said, "Take me to Tahrir Square." Don't ask me why, it wasn't on my to do list nor a place I had hoped to visit. It was more a spur of the moment notion, one of those 'why the hell not?' decisions. So here I was at the home of the Egyptian revolution, Tahrir Square, Cairo, just up from the British Museum containing the mask of Tutankhamun.

I don't speak a word of Arabic outside of 'shukran' meaning 'thank you', 'inshallah' meaning 'God willing' and 'wassalam allekun' meaning 'God and peace be with you.' I walked around the make shift camp site trying to get a feel for the place. A man walked up to me carrying a placard representing a young man's photo. He started speaking and I apologised that I couldn't understand him. A second man offered to translate. The story related to one of his sons, a twin who had been murdered by the state on a protest outside a nearby government building. His name was Mustafa, a 21 year old student. He had been shot in the head by a sniper from the Interior ministry building. His father was demanding justice for his son and said his wife had not left the house since her son's murder a year previously. So this was the price of standing up against Mubarack's dictatorship. This man came here every day to ensure people knew of his sons sacrifice. He asked me to tell the world and I promised I would tell the people in my world which was basically North Belfast, so I wrote an article for the *North Belfast News* that covered his loss.

I wandered about the Square which was basically a protest camp set up on a roundabout, where three major roads converged in downtown Cairo, near the Presidential Palace and government ministries. I saw some young people who looked like students, having a meeting. I saw several older people arguing and two began to fight. I just hung about and fell into the company of three guys who were also there. One starting chatting and I was engaged in conversation with him when a second and third joined in. I saw a makeshift drinks stand and ordered hot tea for four. This is when I received probably the best compliment I could ever wish for. One of the guys said, "Fra, many people come here, they stay for a few minutes, take a photo and move on, but you stay here and meet the people." I was really happy with what he said I felt that a true sign of solidarity was standing with the people.

Kareem was to become my companion for the next few days. He was unemployed, had a little time on his hands and offered to be my guide during my stay in Cairo. My first priority had been locating the Irish embassy. Instead, I had met the revolutionaries and was already planning to attend a protest from Tahrir Square to the Justice ministry building a few blocks away. Kareem made arrangements to meet me at the hotel the next morning and we planned to go the Egyptian museum dedicated to their Nationalist leader. Before we split up he decided to accompany me on the protest march so with camcorder in hand, we joined the protest along with those demanding justice and prosecutions for police crimes, murders, torture, false imprisonment and beatings.

There were no counter-police actions.

I had expected the protest would be met by a cordon of police blocking the road. I was concerned tear gas and violence might be offered by the state and reciprocated by a part of the crowd but in the event I was happy there was no police presence and as a result, the protest remained peaceful. The protestors marched to the Justice ministry chanting denouncements of the regime, all of which I recorded on my camcorder, including me in the middle of it, all smiles. I panned the camera through 360 degrees as I marched beside the leadership. Typical me! Always at the front!

After the protest I chatted to some street vendors. Perhaps it would have been better had I conversed with those on the protest with whom I could have talked about the regional and local politics as things stood at the moment in time.

Day four I met Kareem at my hotel. He said that it was a good hotel in a very safe and secure area of Cairo for travellers. I told him that I thought it was a bit expensive so he advised me he of a cheaper hotel not too far away so I arranged to leave my accommodation for the one he recommended. We used the local taxis which were very cheap, a communal taxi that carried between one and ten people, a converted Hiace van. It hammered through the traffic, like a fairground amusement ride, helter skelter, weaving from lane to lane. I thought these guys could show our Belfast black taxi drivers a thing or two. We took a second taxi to the museum. Kareem had free entry as an Egyptian citizen but I had to pay as a foreign visitor. I felt ok with that. After the museum we headed back to Cairo.

We had lunch in downtown Cairo and I had some Sisha sitting in the shade. With the prices so cheap you could live very well in Cairo for very little. I love value for money and it encourages me to share the wealth. Having bought lunch for Kareem and left a tip we headed back to Tahrir Square where I bought two tee shirts which represented the revolution: a picture of thousands standing together with the date emblazoned on the front, I still wear it from time to time. Kareem advised me not to go Tahrir Square again as there were sporadic fights and thought I might be in danger. I took his advice although really I should have continued my solidarity work. After all, I had met Kareem there at the Square and Mustafa's father. I heard his story and I went on the march! Why do I let people talk me out of things I want to do or into things I don't want to do?

I had self-funded this trip. While Palestine Aid had money in the bank account and the trip was in reference to our work I wouldn't think of charging the cost of this trip to our group and so my mind was drifting back Gaza and how to get in. The tunnels were now my preoccupation. I would take one more day in Cairo then back to Rafah via El Arish and try again to enter where my heart belonged on this trip, with the people of Gaza.

Kareem had a friend in the army who wanted to meet me. I had stayed in the hotel Kareem had recommended which was functional and cheap and it sold beer so I agreed to chat to him.

My last day with Kareem would include some sightseeing in Cairo using the local taxi buses. I had agreed to meet his friend at the hotel. He was an intelligence officer in the Egyptian army who was curious about why I wanted to visit Gaza and support the Palestinian cause. I had nothing to hide and Kareem had been very supportive so I thought, why not? Kareem and I visited a mosque in Cairo, very beautiful and famous. I was getting used to visiting mosques as I'd seen the blue mosque in Istanbul and others previously. As we were leaving the mosque a street hawker approached us. I walked on as I knew what was coming. He spoke with Kareem and Kareem asked if I would like to visit his shop. I declined. The guy spoke again to Kareem and I began to think he might be a friend of Kareem. He asked what we wanted to do. I said I was hungry so he directed us to a restaurant just down the lane, offered us tea and introduced us to his son who had just returned from America. On one level it was very friendly and civil but on another I kept saying to Kareem "I'm not going into his shop." I had no intention of buying anything. I needed nothing. Food was ordered from the restaurant upstairs, a delicious meal, the best I had yet. It comprised of chicken and rice with noodles, an Egyptian speciality.

The shop vendor dropped a few hints, perhaps I would visit inside the shop which was directly facing us, "no pressure" he said. He noticed I was wearing a Palestinian scarf and said he had beautiful silks in store. I knew exactly what he had in store: the hard sell and I was having none of it. As we finished the meal he tried to usher me into the shop. I became quite angry and belligerent. I said "Kareem, there's no way I am going into that shop." I had been consistent all along. I had heard stories that if you go into their shops they lock the door and you don't get out until you have bought enough to make it profitable for them. It may be an urban myth but I wasn't in the mood to test the truthfulness of it.

I asked Kareem if he knew this man and he said he didn't. I asked him why we were there. He said we wanted food and the man had offered to help. We were only being polite. I asked the price of the food and was told 25 Egyptian Pounds maximum. I gave him 50 and said "we will be on our way". 50 Egyptian pounds is about £8. A cheap escape I felt as this barracuda was lining me up for a second suit case full of expensive clothes to take home. Off we went and slowly made our way back to the hotel.

Now these taxi buses are like real buses: they have terminals where they finish. We had a fifteen minute walk to the new hotel and the light was beginning to fade. Kareem's phone rang. It was his army officer friend confirming our appointment. Kareem spoke to him and hung up. I asked what was happening and Kareem explained that he would pick us up at the roadside. I said in no uncertain terms I was not getting into a car with a stranger at the side of the road. Maybe I was being overly cautious but having lived in Belfast and known how many Catholic Irish nationalists the notorious protestant, unionist, loyalist Shankill Butchers had kidnapped off the streets in North Belfast and brutally murdered, people who I believed tried to kidnap myself and my friend when he was just 17 and I was only 15, I thought I would forgo that particular car journey.

A few minutes' walk before reaching our destination and up popped Kareem's friend. Kareem told him I wouldn't get in. The guy's English was very good and perhaps being used to giving commands due to his position in the army, he ordered me to get in. Ten seconds later I had put approximately 30 metres between me and the car. Kareem was calling to me, I stopped. I shouted "I'm not getting into that car."

So Kareem caught up to me and we walked the rest of the way to the hotel. I had gone from perfectly relaxed in Kareem's company to 'there's not a chance in hell you will get me into that car' in under a minute. Call it intuition, self-preservation, experience or anxiety but if I feel it's right no matter the danger I will do it, as self-evidenced by the trip, and if I feel it's wrong, wild horses couldn't make me do it.

Now in the hotel lounge having a beer with Kareem and his friend I chilled out and we had a minor interrogation of sorts. The guy was genuinely interested in my motivation for going to Gaza. It was either professional, personal or both. We chatted about Palestine and I gave them some Irish history about British oppression. I drew the parallels of Ireland under the British, America under the control of white European colonisers and Palestine under Zionist occupation. It was really an enjoyable evening. Good company, intelligent conversation with a few beers. Between the heat of the day, my contracting appetite and the free flowing cheap cold beer I was getting pretty inebriated. I shook both their hands and gave Kareem some money which he refused to take. He said he had wanted to show Cairo to me as a friend. I said I was not offering him money for his services but as a thank you for his kindness so we parted friends. Kareem with the money he hadn't expected to have and me with another friend and memories money couldn't buy.

Next morning I was up early and off to El Arish, the port where we had landed on Viva Palestina 5, a town we had bypassed and never seen, and this would be my new stop off point en route to Gaza, the journey Mark 2. I was neither tired, elated nor exited, I was just determined to try and find a way in.

Kareem and Fra in downtown Cairo

El Arish

Chapter 11

Now it was back to the bus station, this time for a non-transferrable direct bus journey with one stop at the Suez Canal crossing. Now I had done this a few days previously and knew it would be fairly straight forward. A quick look at the passport, check the photo against my face, sniff the bags for drugs or explosives and voila or so I thought!

As we drove over the Suez Canal Bridge I took a few photos from my camera and at the other end we were stopped as I had expected, by the bridge security detail. Again I held up my passport for inspection. A young man seated not too far from me was talking to the soldier and pointing at me. I had no idea what was transpiring but the next thing I knew, the soldier was motioning for me to follow him off the bus. He told me to bring my bags and marched me over the road to the security post. I thought this can't be good as I had been singled out. A simple glance back at the bus showed I was the object of some speculative conversations from my fellow passengers as some had exited the bus and were engaged in chatting and smoking, obviously interested in what was happening to me. A middle aged senior officer came out of the security building. He was either a commando or a para trooper: Very lean, very tall, very fit, very authoritarian and a bit menacing. First he asked me if I had taken photographs of the Suez Canal to which I replied to him that I had. I explained that I was a tourist on holiday, if I was in Paris I would take pictures of the Eiffel Tower but as I was in Egypt and the Suez Canal was renowned the world over, I simply wanted a souvenir. As I was being questioned my bag was being searched. He asked me to show him the photos on my camera that I had taken of the Canal. They discovered my camcorder and asked me to show them what was on it. I remembered my video clip where I was smiling, marching with protestors denouncing the government, demanding arrests of the military and the police. Oops! I thought if they see that he's going to take me round the back of the pillar box and start slapping me. I explained I had only bought the camcorder and had not used it nor did I know how to work it and I prayed the guy playing with it didn't know either.

At the same time I was being asked when I had arrived in Egypt. From memory it was December 26th, St Stephens day.

He asked for my entry visa.

Now I was getting confused, different questions from different people was disorientating me. Perhaps that was the idea, alternate questions impeding my thought process. I asked for my passport back and began looking through it. Bearing in mind I had previous entry stamps from Egypt, The Palestine Authority in Gaza, Syria and Lebanon, it took a few minutes to find the latest entry. There it was on page 17 of my passport.

He asked where I was going and I told him El Arish. I said I was on holiday touring around Egypt. He glanced very closely at the visa entry date then took off his glasses for a better look. Then he let me go on my way. I re-joined those already back on the bus, the last to board. No-one said anything, passed comment or made me feel uncomfortable. A short time later we were in the stop-off restaurant enjoying food, Shisha and a cool drink. Every time people from the bus began to leave the restaurant I was ready to bolt outside but the guy running the restaurant came over and told me to relax and he would let me know when it was time for the bus to depart.

I always found in all my dealings with people in the Middle East a friendliness, compassion and understanding that I rarely find at home. Perhaps we are more grateful for help in environments where we really need it.

Six to seven hours after I left Cairo I found myself in a taxi in El Arish looking for a hotel. Had I known the town centre was only a short walk from the bus station I would probably have walked. Ten minutes after arriving I was checked into a hotel situated above a block of shops. I was tired and drained from the heat and the sun. I headed out for a walk in search of food and found I was staying was on the main Street in El Arish named July 25 Avenue. I found a shop selling crisps, chocolates and juice. I saw a restaurant but not being sure if they spoke English or how much the food would cost or indeed what was on the menu, I just had snacks for dinner. I had a cold shower in the hotel because they only had cold water from what I could tell and there were no towels. I only realised this when I stepped into the shower and there was no soap either so I had a cold shower and drip dried on top of the bed. There was a lot of shouting in a neighbouring room and it sounded violent. A vicious argument with raised voices, even the language barrier could not disguise an angry exchange.

Chatting with the owner the next day I explained I was trying to get to Gaza and might use the tunnels. He explained that he had a friend, a taxi driver, who might be able to help. A plan was hatched. I went in search of an Internet café and walked into a small shopping mall adjacent to my hotel. I walked around a bit, building up the courage to approach someone. I walked into an electronic shop and asked if there was an internet café nearby. The assistant understood my request for Wi-Fi and brought me to a perfume shop that was close. I thought "here we go he's trying to get me to buy after shave and perfume." I thought, "Just play this out and ask for an internet café." I needed to confirm to my friends in Gaza I was in El Arish and making plans to visit them. I needed someone to meet me in the event that I used the tunnels. I couldn't just pop up in Gaza through a tunnel and walk aimlessly about. As a foreigner I might be viewed as a spy or undesirable.

The guy in the perfume shop asked me how long I wanted to use the internet for. It was on the tip of my tongue to say "why is that important, I just want the internet." In the end I just gave in and said "I don't know, maybe 30 minutes to catch up with friends?" He beckoned me behind the counter, showed me his laptop and said "it's online, help yourself." There and then began a friendship with the owner. He asked the same questions that I had heard before like why was I interested in Palestine? It transpired his father was Palestinian, a teacher by profession and his mother was Egyptian. He promised to help in any way he could and invited me to call to the shop the next day for lunch.

The periods of being on my own in the hotel, on the bus etc were being very well compensated by people freely offering to help, so I chatted for maybe two hours after I'd finished messaging Pauline and Yousef. I was in contact with Julie from New Zealand who had been on the convoy and presently still resident in Gaza. I phoned her from a pay phone in the El Arish post office. She had given me her number via social media.

Day one in El Arish had gone better than I had hoped. On day two I would meet the taxi driver and lunch with Hassan turned out to be a five course meal where I was taken to his family home and introduced to his father. Such hospitality was welcome and unexpected, I was very grateful. I was counting the days from when I had arrived. St Stephen's Day, December 26th. This was now day six possibly seven and the available time to visit Gaza was fast running out. I met the taxi driver and he agreed to take me to the border the next day so I packed the few belongings I had brought and met him early. I thanked the hotel owner for his assistance and headed off to Rafah.

The driver didn't speak English but kept looking in my eyes and pointing to them. I think he found my blue eyes fascinating. I have deep blue eyes while most Palestinians and Egyptians have brown eyes. As we neared Rafah town not far from the border post, he got on his mobile phone and started talking. Suddenly a man came out of the shadows holding a phone to his ear and waving to us. Not for the first time I felt everything was surreal, like in a film. The driver asked me for the telephone number of my friend Yousef who was meeting me in Gaza. I gave him the number, he dialled Yousef and they chatted briefly before he handed me the phone. Yousef said there were some complications. No-one can arrive unannounced at the tunnels. It's ok for Palestinians but as a foreigner I needed someone to vouch for me and the Gazan authorities, in this case Hamas, had to agree.

So here I was for the second time at the border being refused entry: the first time at the official entrance and now at the unofficial entrance. I had no option but to return, not to Cairo this time, but to El Arish.

Yousef promised to smooth things out for me and the driver offered to take me back. There were people trying to hail our taxi so he asked me if I wanted to share the taxi. I declined so he hammered on back towards El Arish passing through the check point on leaving Rafah. This time we were not waved through but pulled over. The driver showed his identification papers while I was asked for my passport. The guard disappeared and I waited patiently for his return. He was a young man in his late teens or early twenties. He had dark plastic sunglasses and was wearing a black Crombie style jacket. I thought he looked like an extra from *Blues Brothers*. Standing there in a world of my own I was startled when someone rapped heavily on the outside window of the passenger's side and asked me to step out of the car. This was a different guy who spoke excellent English. He asked me where I had been and I told him I'd been to visit Rafah. He wanted to know why so I told him it was close to where I was staying. He asked me where that was so I said "El Arish." He then asked me when I arrived in Egypt so I thought "here we go again." I replied that I had arrived on December 26th so he asked me to show him my entry visa. I went straight to page 17 on my Passport having had this conversation previously at the Suez Canal. He looked at the entry visa and said "my friend, we have a problem." I said "what kind of a problem?"

He showed me the entry visa and I had to agree with him that it was very faint and difficult to see. He then explained that his colleague had failed to see my entry visa and thought I was travelling without a valid entry visa in Egypt and had perhaps entered illegally for unknown purposes.

He had phoned his superior commander in the intelligence service and they now had orders to search the car and asked if I minded? I told him that it was the driver's car and it was between him and the driver.

Now, if you remember, I told this guy I was staying in El Arish and only sightseeing in Rafah. It became obvious I was being deceitful when they opened the trunk and found my suitcases. Before I had left Belfast some Palestinian Activists at the Royal Victoria Hospital had donated some dialysis catheters to be forwarded to the local Nephrology renal unit. I had carried these all the way from home. The soldier showed them to my interrogator. I quickly said they had been donated by a charity back home for an Egyptian hospital. To be fair I think the guy knew I was either coming from or going to Gaza.

Next they found my tripod stand. I made a school boy error .I offered information they hadn't requested. I said "that's a tripod stand for my camera." "Oh, you have a camera, may we see it?"

132

To my eternal shame, once I'd gotten to El Arish I had erased all the photos and video taken in Cairo. The footage I had would have made the hair stand on the back of your head. I had been concerned when stopped on the Suez Canal by the military. Anti-government rallies featuring me would not help me at these check points so I had deleted it. At least in this case I had nothing to worry about. The cameras were in my shoulder bag and my shoulder bag was behind my seat unseen between the seat and the back seat. On showing them the camera and my shoulder bag, they had uncovered my guilty secret. The reason I had been anxious on this journey was about to be revealed.

With the problems transferring the cash electronically from Belfast to Gaza, the whole reason for this trip was to deliver the money. The soldier took out €3,500 from my back pack. I thought perfect! This is just what you would carry if you were a spy, a huge amount of cash to pay for bribes or informants. I thought "this is it Fra, they're going to arrest and or question you at length." To his credit, while the soldier looked incredulous and suspicious in equal measure the young guy asked me if the money was mine. I replied that it was and he said to the soldier, "it's ok, it's his money put it back."

He then slowly handed me back my passport and said "my friend, will you do me a favour?" I asked what that favour could be and he said "next time you visit Egypt, be sure to check your visa stamp and make sure it's visible, otherwise it may cause you problems." I shook his hand to show I held no malice, he gave me a smile, looked at the driver, nodded to the car and off we went at 90 mph back to El Arish.

I don't know who was more relieved, the driver or me. If I'd said he had taken me to the tunnels he would probably have been questioned and beaten and I would have been arrested. It was just as well all my details were in order, I had been temporarily detained, unnecessarily. It was a good result for us both.

He dropped me off back at the hotel. We agreed to try again once I got permission. I now had three days left before I went back to Cairo and onward to Sharm El Sheik.

I called in to see Ramez Ibrahim in the perfume shop. He was confused to see me. I explained the complications and he understood. He asked me where I was staying and I told him I was going to check into a hotel but not the one I had previously stayed in. He said "please, be my guest, come and stay with me." That night I slept in his spare room. My best night's sleep so far, relaxed in a real home with someone I trusted.

Next day it was confirmed, I could go to Gaza via the tunnels. At most I'd have forty eight hours or less, probably less as I had to be in El Arish early on my day of departure for the long trip to Cairo. I'd really need to leave the night before so that would cut down my visit to just over one day. I had come all this way, spent so much time, effort, money and emotion on the chance to get in for one day. It was almost an anti-climax. I chatted to Ramez. He asked why I was so determined to get to Gaza. I told him about the money I was carrying and he asked to see it. I thought "no going back now" so I showed him the money. He asked what my priority was and I told him it was to get the money to the university for the scholarship. Everything else was secondary.

He said "tomorrow I will meet my mother at the border. Do you trust me?" I said I did, with no hesitation. This man had helped me, offered his hospitality and a roof over my head and asked for nothing in return. He said "tomorrow we go to the border. I will look out for someone I know, you give them the money for the university. Then we contact the university and if the money is not handed over, I will give Hamas the passport number and name of the friend we use." I thought, "well, I can't take it home." I would trust Hassan.
That night I was in contact with friends in Gaza. They were disappointed I was not using the tunnel. I said it was too big a risk

for 24 hours, to be caught by the border guards. I explained I would get the money in via a courier and explained the plan.

My friends in Gaza didn't know my new friend in El Arish and as such it became pretty clear they didn't trust Hassan because they didn't know him and the money I carried in cash was a very large amount. So plan B was discussed. If I could not get through the tunnel to Gaza perhaps one of them could come and meet me in Rafah. I explained this idea to my friend from the perfume shop. Initially he was hesitant and I realised that there's no trust between these guys because they didn't know each other.

He asked me if I knew this person in Gaza well and if I trusted them. I told him that they had been part of the official delegation that welcomed Viva Palestina 5 to Gaza in 2010 and I did trust them. So it was agreed. Someone from Gaza would come and meet us in Rafah. The arrangements had been made. We would simply select a time that suited both parties.

We travelled by car through the military security checkpoint at Rafah and drove down the same road I had travelled by taxi towards the tunnels previously. Then we waited. We were meant to meet around 4pm and by 6pm I was getting concerned then the phone rang and there was our contact.

My friend in his perfume shop, El Arīsh, Egypt.

Getting The Money In

Chapter 12

Still brushing sand from his shoulders he appeared from nowhere and we moved forward to greet him. I must say it was fantastic to see him after all the problems I'd endured to get this far. We adjourned to a nearby coffee shop to drink tea and smoke Sisha! I still wonder at times how far I'd come on my personal journey that led me to meet these guys, clandestine almost; the risk my friend from Gaza had taken; all of us glad to be in each others company; all agreed the money was of paramount importance; the aim, to help someone in their studies and promote solidarity.

We chatted for about two hours before I noticed that our friend from Gaza was getting a bit anxious. It was the first time since the siege began that he had left Gaza. It was hard to believe I had travelled several thousand miles through different countries and borders and he couldn't travel fifty metres into Egypt. This really put things back into perspective for me.

Now it was time for him to travel back via the tunnels but there was a complication. He did not have any money and he had to pay the tunnel toll. He had promised the people who operate the tunnels that he would pay them on his return. He had been allowed through on the strength of it and he had to leave his ID papers with them as proof of his bona fide intentions. My friend from El Arish thought that as it was his idea to come that he should pay the toll and that as I was a visitor and guest, I should not be obliged to make the payment. It was $100 for me to go via the tunnels as a foreigner and $50 for locals. I said in the grand scheme of things that I was happy to pay the toll and it was worth it to both see him and know the money would be safely transported to the university. It wouldn't be right to take the money from the scholarship as that had been raised through voluntary donations. I paid the $50 which we agreed in Egyptian pounds and off my companion went back to life under siege. 1.8 million souls living in a place 25 miles by 6 miles, the most densely populated place on earth, constantly under blockade and occasional deadly bombardment. Nowhere to run, nowhere to hide, no bomb shelters, no army, no air force, no navy and no-one else in the world to protect them. I didn't envy him. I just felt for all those in Gaza who live under Zionist military control who could be shot, bombed, maimed or killed at any moment.

All I asked was a confirmation email from the university from their email address which I already had and from the person, with whom I had already agreed the scholarship, that all the monies had been received and I needed a receipt for Palestine Aid accounts. In the end I not only got the confirmation email but a photo too of the money being handed over. I was well pleased.

Job done I could finally relax.

I spent my last day in El Arish with my friend, as his guest. The following morning he took me to the bus station and I made my way back to Cairo. I had brought some gifts for my friends in Gaza from Belfast, baseball caps with Ireland or shamrocks emblazoned on them, key rings, tee shirts and one or two hoodies. I thought I would leave them on the bed in my friend's apartment for him to find once I'd left. I thanked him for his hospitality, friendship and help and sat back relaxing on the bus as I headed to Cairo en route to Sharm el Shiek and Pauline.

I had booked one night in the Sunshine Hostel, Cairo near to Tahrir Square. The booking referral site write ups were encouraging. It was in downtown Cairo so no travelling in and out of the city and hopefully I would find the bus station I needed to get the bus to Sharm and meet up with Pauline. The journey is never uneventful. As we neared Cairo I began to question where I should alight and how I would get to my destination. The bus just appeared to stop, not in the bus station but out on a hill overlooking the city. It's really a huge place like Istanbul heaving with humanity, manic traffic and huge crowds. I asked someone on the bus for advice. They said most people get off the bus here as it was handy for the town. I'm not sure it was a proper bus stop or more a convenience stop for those travelling into the centre. Perhaps it avoided the traffic congestion or the bus terminal wasn't really in the centre so off I got and followed the crowd into Cairo - no GPS on my phone and no internet credit on my mobile.

Here we go again. I took a deep breath and went to find someone who hopefully spoke English and to get directions. I had purposefully booked my accommodation near Tahrir Square hoping to revisit the solidarity protest camp so I asked for directions to there. Wherever I ended up, it wasn't that far away. I got to the Square, asked a street vendor for further directions, and five minutes later I was walking up the stairs of what appeared to be a semi derelict building. My hopes shattered as I questioned my choice of where I had reserved to stay. I was literally having reservations about my reservation. I was already considering moving as I entered a very old, dilapidated lift and ascended to the second floor. However, the place was really nice inside confirming what I'd read. It reminded of the hostels or hotels you sometimes find in Europe, pensions or apartment blocks where some of the apartments had been bought to be used as tourist accommodation while others were still privately owned.

The hostel was split over two floors. I found my private room and then joined a few others that were in the communal living area lying on the cushioned floor enjoying tea. Was I dreaming? I was surprised at how confident I felt because usually I don't like putting myself under pressure to converse with strangers outside of the usual pleasantries. I have learned that travelling alone forces me to be more outgoing and sociable otherwise the world can be a very lonely place.

I met a Scottish guy and an English woman both travelling separately who had met up on the road somewhere and had decided to travel together for a while. He confided in me that he had enough to do watching out for and taking care of himself without having to worry about her safety too. The extra responsibility was unwelcome although he was quite tall, fit and looked like he could handle himself. It reassured me a bit that I wasn't being overly anxious when I too at times was very conscious of the fact that I was a white monied European walking about a city in which millions lived on just $2 a day and many more in absolute poverty. I was travelling the next day and enquired where I would get the bus to Sharm. The response came, "look out the window, that's it there, at the roundabout." Result!

I walked across the road with three lane traffic in each direction and bought my ticket for the 10am coach direct to Sharm el Sheik. Back at the hostel I wanted to upload some photos from my laptop and asked about Wi-Fi. It transpired it was in the other part of the hostel on the upper floor so I went upstairs, asked for the code and attempted to upload my photos. I have no experience or skill in doing that and I must have tried for thirty minutes. In the end, frustrated by my lack of progress, I asked the young guy behind reception for his help. I am a firm believer that if you give a 10 year old an android phone today he could probably hack NASA given enough time.

This young Egyptian guy opened or created a file for my photos and hey presto, two minutes later I was whizzing through my portfolio and selecting pictures to share on social media, specifically Facebook. We got to chatting and he asked why I was visiting Cairo, a fairly innocuous, straight forward question. I considered what to say - a business trip, just passing through to Sharm or the truth. Remember, the truth will set us free, but it can also get us into trouble when others don't share our political outlook. I looked at him for a moment and told him I had tried to get into Gaza and related the story pretty much as described here.

He showed me his screen saver. He had been on his laptop all the time I had been trying to upload my photos and on his laptop was a photo. Really iconic stuff. A young man sitting in the road, head covered, surrounded by tear gas, giving the global sign of resistance, the peace sign of two fingers turned towards the aggressor. It was a fantastic photo - something you might see on the cover of *Time Magazine*. I told him that I thought it was a tremendous photograph. His reply shocked me. "That's me" he said. Yet again by intuition, guidance or pure blind luck, I had met a fellow activist.

I told him about my visits to Tahrir Square and the march to the justice ministry. He asked if I had introduced myself to the revolutionaries. I said that I hadn't as I hadn't wanted to turn up and just assume people would make time for me. He said he would pass on my solidarity greetings and wished me a safe journey to Sharm.

Next day bright and early I boarded the air conditioned coach, much more comfortable than the other public transport buses I'd used and went several hours down to the coast. From the bus station I took a taxi to my hotel for my all-inclusive two week break by the sea. When I arrived I got reception to call Pauline in her room and she came down to meet me. Her journey had been uneventful although she was travelling alone not knowing when I would arrive.

March to the Justice Ministry Cairo

Relaxing At Last

Chapter 13

Next day we met Chris, one of the diving instructors, a really great guy and a true gentleman. We fell into conversation. He mentioned he was from Cairo and I told him I'd just been there. Next thing I was telling him the story about my travels. I mentioned the two tee shirts I had bought from Tahrir Square. He said "do me a favour, you and Pauline put them on and meet me at the diving reception point." We dutifully obliged and Chris met us with two friends who wanted photos with the guy from Belfast who travelled to Gaza via revolutionary Tahrir Square.

The holiday was great, good weather, the food passable, free but not very strong alcohol and the beach on our door steps. We left our hotel a few times to get into another part of the resort that had restaurants, shops, dive shops, internet and bars. At one of these places there was a map on the ground like a mosaic showing the surrounding areas. As I looked I saw Rafah. I showed a shop seller the map and asked "is that Rafah near Gaza?" He said it was and I asked him how far it was. He said it was around an hour by taxi. I thought, "but I have just travelled several hours up to Cairo, stayed over and travelled all the way down, when Gaza was only an hour or two away." I had to laugh!

Camel riding, snorkelling and another trip back to Cairo, this time by plane, to see the Pyramids with Pauline were my other highlights: all in all another unforgettable journey.

Stop over point on the Suez Canal en route to El Arīsh

Part 5

Bradford to Gaza:
The journey moves on

Chapter 14

My next sojourn on my walk with Palestine was a continuation of my solidarity work. My friend from London Carole Swords, former participant on Viva Palestina 5 and the Beirut summer camp, advised me of another Gaza bound convoy leaving from Bradford. I had neither the time nor the money nor the support to try and fundraise at short notice to get supplies and to get a vehicle on the road but I did contact the organisers offering my services as a relief driver. My commitment was to pay for my own accommodation, food, essentials and fares to Britain and back from Gaza and drive a vehicle as part of a team if they needed drivers. It was all I could afford due to the short time frame of the convoy's departure and I felt even if I didn't get a place on the convoy, yet again I had shown a willingness to stand up and be counted in supporting the people of Gaza and Palestine.

Initially I was informed they had enough people going but soon thereafter things began to change.

Once the route had been decided that the convoy would take there was some confusion and some dissent. Not being a member of the convoy at this time I was unaware of many of these doubts cast by some who may have agreed in principle or indeed fact, to join the convoy. This time the Convoy entitled 'Bradford to Gaza Viva Palestina Arabia' was a joint venture being organised in Britain and in the Middle East. Our route would take us through Syria which was in the middle of a contrived civil war or a process of destabilisation used for the purposes of regime change to favour the West, Israel and the Gulf States.

Herein lay the problem.

The major concerns from the first convoy were the inherent danger of staying in Gaza which was being regularly and summarily bombed by Israel. Now this convoy from Bradford to Gaza had chosen to travel through Syria. Seriously, these were dangerous times for all those living in Syria and anyone travelling through it. Would the convoy be a high value target for kidnapping or destruction? These were serious, worrying concerns which I felt I really had to mull over in my mind. Never one to make rash impulsive decisions and always determined to see them through I spent a few days thinking. I mentioned it to Pauline and several others - the consensus was not to do it. It was too dangerous.

I felt it was a daily risk for all those in Syria and Palestine. Had not the people of Latakia welcomed us? Perhaps we would billet there again. Was it cowardice or common sense not to go through Syria, was there an alternative route? Well as you can probably guess, I sat down, thought it through and decided solidarity is not a soft option, it's a firm commitment. I was going! The decision was made for better or worse, I'd see it through. So with money in my current account to cover my expenses, van insurance for the trip and a new international driving licence, I boarded a flight to Leeds Bradford to be met by Amar at the airport and a new Odyssey had begun.

Amar was a great guy, a British born national of Pakistani heritage. He took me for food then to my hotel where I had booked in for a few days. I collected the van, a blue transit, with the logo 'Bradford to Gaza' emblazoned on the side and a heart shaped Union Jack. Now I'm not a fan of the 'Butchers Apron' as many refer to the

Union Jack but it was their convoy and I was a driver on that convoy so there were no complaints from me but a few quips from the boys and girls back home.

We gathered donations of food and clothes from the local mainly though not exclusively Muslim community of Bradford. We had the vehicles gather in a car park in Bradford, where George Galloway had stood for election to Westminster. After a rousing send-off we headed down the motorway to London. Back on the road again!

We were directed to North London for our first nights stop over where I met those joining us from London on the trip. We slept on the floor of a community centre and my only plan the next morning before departure was to buy an AC/ DC transformer so I could charge the batteries for my camera phone and laptop while driving. Job done, we headed for the Channel Tunnel. This was a completely different experience already and we had just begun our sojourn: no other Irish on the convoy; numbers drastically reduced; and a feeling of uncertainty of what lay ahead.

I'm not sure how many vehicles we had maybe ten or twelve. We had one of the convoy leaders from before, Amer, Carole Swords from London, and others joined us from previous convoys but for many this was their first experience. The route this time would be different, no Paris, Lyon or Milan. This journey would mirror many convoys that go to Afghanistan, Kashmir or Pakistan. We would go first to Calais then Belgium, Austria, Germany, Romania, Hungary, Turkey, Syria, Jordan then Palestine. So our second night was spent in our vans in a car park in Calais having taken the train from the UK.

Early the next the day we drove to Belgium and stayed in a small quirky roadside motel. The first convoy had been very disciplined; people were involved; committed; and determined. This convoy was more individual, less structured and at times belligerent. The main difference I have to conclude was the level of solidarity amount the participants. Perhaps I'd been spoiled having been part of a more organised group, perhaps having no organised groups made this campaign more individualistic. It would prove to be troublesome as the days ahead turned into weeks.

My first inkling of any dissent came from an older member of the convoy. This person wanted the convoy to go into the town centres to raise the profile and let us be seen as had been done on previous occasions. I felt slightly disappointed that this was not going to be the case but my philosophy was to do what the organisers had planned. This wasn't a democratic 'what shall we do today convoy, make it up as you go along adventure.' We had all agreed to join a convoy organised by Viva Palestina Arabia and we should follow their lead literally and follow their instructions. If you want to do your own thing then organise your own convoy!

I won't say that I am a good judge of character but I know bad news when I see it and here it was standing in front of me - a classic saboteur. This person tasked me and a young guy from London to go to Amer, the co-ordinator, and tell him we wanted to parade our vehicles through the town. I just said "if you'd like that to happen then perhaps you would like to mention that to Amer yourself?" It was a classic example of one person making the snow balls or loading the guns but getting other people to fire them.

This was not going to be fun and I had a foreboding about this person's presence on the convoy. On my first convoy to Gaza I had been advised to make notes and complete a dairy of the journey which I neglected to do, mainly because my focus was on the trip and realising my goal of getting to Gaza. This time I brought a camcorder to record the trip. I began my first recording with a young female participant from America. I asked things like what her expectations, fears and hopes were for the days ahead? I found it a great way to actually chat to people on the convoy and to get to know them and see glimpses of the real person behind their convoy persona and the real reasons why they were on this

149

journey. In every case I met and interviewed people standing against injustice, standing up for Palestine, for humanitarian relief and against apartheid Israel. It wasn't Muslims defending Muslims it was people defending strangers who were just other people, a real tonic for the soul. No wild political idealism nor misplaced religious fervour, just ordinary people like you and me standing up for humanity. Next we went to Luxembourg and seeing all the different destinations as we went through them and on the road signs marking down how many miles to our next town or city was exciting. I had never been in many of these places or countries before. It was all a very new and welcome experience and again the weather was sublime. This was to be a land convoy through Europe.

When we got to Luxembourg we got lost, very easily done! Even though we had a few walkie talkies throughout the convoy and CB radios to keep the convoy intact, it only took a missed turn or a red light or a misread sign for people to go left instead of right or uphill instead of downhill or to wait until the traffic lights changed. Half an hour went by while people got directions, turned on sat navs or google maps and we met up again by a war memorial in the town centre. A short stop for photos but no time for sightseeing and off we went again.

We began to settle into the daily routine of convoy life. Breakfast early, hit the road, travel all day, camp early, shower, food, petrol, check the van, beer if you wanted it, sleep in the van or at a camping site or a hotel en route. It worked pretty well, the weather was fantastic, listening to Rovics on the CD, Pol Mac Adaim and a few rebel tunes, Following the van in front, pretty relaxing and good company at the end of the night.

I was glad I was travelling alone on this convoy. When you have a travel companion I think it creates its own dynamics and comfort zone. Alone on the convoy I had to reach out to other people, make a greater effort to mingle and it made the journey more appealing and in some aspects more rewarding: different people, different conversations, different opinions and different outlooks. Yeah, very refreshing and enjoyable.

I met a guy from outside Birmingham, a real gentleman he'd been on many trips to Palestine and further afield, Brother Yousef. He had a dentist's chair and equipment in the back of his van. He had it overloaded by a couple of hundreds of pounds in weight. I was amazed the axle took the strain. He told me that he had personally delivered over £500,000 worth of aid in monetary value, I believed him when he showed me what was in the van. Never under estimate the value of one committed individual. That's a remarkable personal achievement for an individual and I salute his bravery and steadfastness. He's probably still doing it, unassuming, not looking for reward or favour, recognition or titles, just getting on with doing the right thing. Priceless!

I started to form a bond of friendship with Richard. He had been on previous convoys but this was the first time we had travelled together. He was a professional magician, a children's entertainer and performed in many different arenas and theatres throughout the country. An Englishman living in Wales he proudly flew the Welsh dragon from his bus on the convoy. As we were both of a certain vintage and to keep down the hotel expenses, we shared a room on the nights the convoy chose hotel accommodation. We had a beer, ate lightly and chatted about his father, ex British forces who had served in Yemen and Richard related memories of growing up there while his father was stationed in Sanna. As I am by my politics anti-colonial and anti-imperialist, it was interesting to have these conversations without it descending into an argument about exploitation, invasion and occupation but as Richard was on the convoy which on some level confronted Israeli occupation, exploitation and colonisation of Palestine, we were on the same the wave length.

The person who I thought to be trouble for the convoy was also on good terms with Richard and a distancing between ourselves would enter the relationship later in the journey. I liked Richard but this other person was not on my fraternising list.

So days turned into a week and we headed through Austria and into Germany.

We visited Cologne staying in a camp outside the town. Jeminah from Malaysia, her travelling companion and I drove into the city for dinner and some sightseeing. I had met Jeminah on Viva Palestina 5 and having some things in common like shared memories made her easy company. We saw the old Cathedral, walked the narrow walled streets, bought some ice cream and saw a beautiful young German woman who worked in the town. We strolled along the canal and had Sisha which I didn't think we would have access to outside of the Middle East. After a great night we headed back to camp and I was enjoying the different sights, sounds, conversations and experiences.

Each day or evening we had a quick convoy update concerning where we would be travelling to the next day, how many miles we would cover, how long it would take before we arrived and possible dangers or worries ahead. Those were halcyon days but I might be wearing my rose tinted glasses.

So to refresh - we had guys from Bradford, Birmingham, London, Bristol and Belfast, all individuals although some people knew each other and some had previous convoy experience. We got lost more than once as we travelled through Europe and sometimes the problems we were facing were bad light, bad signage and tiredness. This caused one or two moments of friction and confrontation. It was a waste of energy arguing and at one point a few blows were exchanged through frustration, but hey, these things happen, people get lost, it's not what happens but how you deal with it that matters. This is an example of how convoys differ with different dynamics, different personas and different attitudes.

At one point I became uncomfortable as I genuinely felt one person was causing tension between convoy members and the organisational team. Rather than play games, take sides or get involved I decided to distance myself from the convoy, go to the joint meetings but step back from the social contact. I thought it would make the rest of the journey quite uncomfortable, isolating and lonely. But the pot was being stirred and I was having none of it.

I made my decision much like I had in Belfast. I would batten down the hatches, keep to myself and see it through. I had missed one breakfast and one evening meal when I was approached by another convoy member asking what was wrong. I didn't think my actions would be noticed just so quickly. I said I was uncomfortable with the undercurrent in the convoy and felt attempts were being made to disrupt the convoy and I didn't want any part of that. I wanted to get aid to Gaza and that was my first and only priority.

To give the convoy leaders their due, they acted later that day, they called a convoy meeting saying that if anyone didn't want to be on the convoy they should leave and anyone suspected of undermining the convoy would be left behind and put off the convoy. They had contacted the main organisers in London and related their instructions. The atmosphere changed overnight. I cannot say I felt vindicated but the air was cleared and everyone seemed to make a bigger effort to get along. Finally we had a convoy of the committed or so I thought!

Each day brought new opportunities for meeting the convoy members via my camcorder blog. Each day on the road meant chatting sometimes to the first person you saw after you woke up, had tea with, find the showers with or break bread with. These small personal interactive chats were the backbone of the journey and allowed us all to meet, greet and get along.

After Germany it was Hungary and Romania and I remember the sprawling undulating countryside, mile after mile of unspoiled cultivated farmland, spectacular awe-inspiring scenery. I must go back and revisit the plains of Hungary and Romania. Budapest was fantastic. We stopped on a camp site outside the town. We arrived late in the evening and Jemima, her companion and I jumped in my van and went off to see the sights. It was beautiful at night, the monuments lit up, the old buses and some old Eastern European cars, like travelling back in time.

I wasn't sure what time we were leaving the next day so as some headed into Budapest centre early in the morning I stayed behind with some others to clean out the vans, repack our donated clothes and food, clean my clothes and chill out. All those previous days were really non-stop travelling. This was a rest day so I rested. When the guys came back and told us what a great time they had I thought maybe I should have made the most of the opportunity but I wasn't on holiday, it wasn't a jolly, I was still focussed on Gaza.

We set off for Romania and its capital Bucharest. We were told to be careful on the road and not to pick up hitch hikers. We were told stories of how truckers would pick up female hitchhikers or they would approach the truck while it was stationary at night and the drivers would be robbed. This was the only time we were told to be careful of our safety throughout the trip. I am not casting aspersions on the Romanian people. I felt the convoy leaders were being over protective and relaying stories they had heard but not witnessed. Anyway, we drove thirteen hours straight from one capital to the other, no stops for food or petrol, just a toilet break and for prayers at the side of the road. It's amazing as I write this story how much floods back through association. When I remember the prayer stops in Romania I remember we had previous stops all the way through the convoy. Some of the convoy members were Sunni and some were Shia. We stopped according to the time of day for prayer. Some wanted as many as four prayer breaks. Fine if you're a Muslim adhering to your religious beliefs but a bit overburdening for those who are not. So after a few days it was agreed under certain conditions it was permissible for Muslims when travelling to miss some prayers so long as they prayed at the very moment that day's journey ended. We had actually lost two of the brothers for several hours one night when they stopped for prayers as the convoy continued. When they tried to catch us up they went the wrong way and we all had to circle back.

I mustn't forget Babagee and his companion Mohammed Ali from London. They were part of the organisational team, two great guys, very easy to get along with, relaxed and good company. Babagee was not his real name but a term of endearment for a much loved father type figure. We had many good conversations as at times we were halted here and there at the side of the road and they would walk along the convoy chatting and putting people at ease.

Late at night we found our hotel in Sofia, parked up the vehicle in its patrolled car park and had a great night's sleep in a warm bed, had a hot shower and a decent shave, God it was good to feel alive again. I must say I never felt anything like home sickness, over-whelmed by what we were trying to achieve or down hearted at any stage, just a growing tiredness from the endless driving, the interrupted sleep and general fatigue. I was probably dehydrated too but these rest days were really necessary. And so onto Turkey where we needed to get travel visas, new vehicle insurance and a customs inspection before entry.

We were met again in Turkey by those who supported our aim of reaching Gaza. It was a quite muted greeting, not endorsed by IHH the Turkish humanitarian aid group. We drove straight to Istanbul. I got separated from the group when I was delayed at traffic lights and went under a bridge instead of over it. I found myself at the Blue Mosque with one other vehicle. We couldn't find the rest of the convoy and had not been given the address of our hotel. After several hours we got a phone call telling us where everyone else was. Having no sat navs we followed a taxi to our hotel and parked the vehicles in a nearby underground warehouse. Ah, Istanbul previously known as Constantinople is a beautiful city. We would have two days there. The following morning we had breakfast in the hotel and were joined by Kevin Ovendun from Viva Palestina London.

There had been continued misgivings and grumblings from some on the convoy. Obviously my refusal to get involved in petty personality conflicts had led to my failing to notice realignment on the convoy. Kevin called for a convoy meeting for the following morning. I assumed it was another briefing about going forward this time to Syria. I spent the day wandering the grand bazar in Istanbul. I bought myself a belt as I had lost weight, a jewellery box for Pauline and a compact cosmetic mirror. I chatted with Carole, Babagee and Mohammed and enjoyed a flea market and the sunshine. Later that night I had dinner and beer with Richard and as we walked around town some guys invited us to a brothel. I was tempted just to see what it was like having never been in one but we decided to give it a miss. None of us realised we were staying in the heart of the red light district. This caused some consternation for some of the brothers who were upset by this set of circumstances.

On the morning of departure we had our convoy meeting and an obvious schism had developed. While some of us gathered for breakfast it became apparent others were congregated in one of the hotel rooms making their own decisions about how they would proceed. There was my old friend leading the rebellion, still making the snowballs for others to fire. The phrase 'Lions led by Donkeys' was being repeated several times. I thought the convoy had come together when in fact it has fractured into two camps: those supporting the organisers and those siding with our malcontent. A few studiously stayed independent.

When we came to leave Istanbul for Syria we left about a third of the convoy behind. I am not sure if the defection of one convoy member at the Romanian Turkish border who had decided Syria was a country too far for him had an effect on others in the convoy or if the spirit of undermining the organisers had infected many but there by the port we separated and went our different ways. All the vehicles were transferred over to Viva Palestina so the aid could travel on to Gaza. New drivers were allocated from the existing pool of people staying on and would take charge of these vans.

I was disappointed having travelled all that way together, to lose people now. I was even more disappointed when I noticed the object of all the perceived dissent was staying on the convoy. Encouraging others perhaps to leave but staying on themselves. We fired up our engines and headed to Syria.

Bradford to Gaza convoy, leaving for London: Gaza bound.

Syria

Chapter 15

We would be delayed by several hours amid attempts to force us to use a different crossing point. Bearing in mind Syria was in the grip of a civil war or a war conceived, funded and financed in Washington, Tel Aviv, Riyadh and Istanbul for the Balkanisation of Syria or regime change to favour Western and regional objectives in the proxy war against Hezbollah and Iran, it wasn't only the weather that was hotting up.

We found ourselves at the Turkish Syrian border on a sweltering hot afternoon. At first we were told we couldn't cross at this border crossing as it was primarily for commercial traffic like heavy goods lorries.

I knew this was a different crossing from before but the organisers refused to move as the next crossing was many miles away but more importantly a delegation of Syrian officials was waiting for us on the other side. There were several delays and a few nervous moments as the trucks were scanned by X-ray machines and one or two randomly searched. Eventually, after what seemed like an eternity we were allowed to proceed. Our reception was very warm on the Syrian side of the border but very much a low key affair. We were greeted by the local state dignitaries, posed for pictures and had some refreshments. I wasn't sure where exactly in Syria we would be staying. I had hoped it might be Latakia bringing back memories of the previous convoy but I knew Latakia had been attacked by that seeking regime change. I looked at our hosts and wondered how many of these secular officials defending the Syrian Arab Republic would survive the conflict. Every person in front of me would be a target and a prized kill for those they stood against. I wondered how many had already suffered, lost loved ones or had sons or daughters in the Syrian Arab Army defending the Republic. A state brought into being after fighting a national war of independence against its colonial French occupier. I was glad my travels through Syria would be short lived and safe. I wonder how many of those courageous people I met are still alive.

With hindsight I feel the crossing the Syrians directed us to was carefully chosen. Not too much civilian traffic and used less frequently than many of the other crossings. Parts of Syria bordering Turkey were already in the hands of the fundamentalists. It has come to light that Turkey was already facilitating arming and funding these murderous gangs and that may partly explain the difficulties we encountered in crossing the border.

Now that we were ready to proceed, we were joined by our escort. Previously it had been one or two Police cars leading us on the motorways but this was different. We had a heavily armed escort: men with machine guns in vehicles at the front, in the middle and at the back of the convoy. We had our escort then three convoy vehicles then an escort and so on.

I recalled the worries expressed by many before we entered Syria that we might be high value assets for kidnapping or ambush as some saw us as supporting the regime. My focus was always on Gaza and as those who fought Assad did so on behalf of the West; I have to confess, if I was asked, I would say I supported the secular government of Syria defending the Republic against religious fundamentalists and those willing to destroy Syria for the benefit of Israel, the Gulf States and the West. So, with an armed escort we set off at speed for our first port of call, Tartous, on the Syrian coastline. One or two people had left the convoy as the danger of travelling through Syria grew in their minds. For those who braved the journey the bonds of friendship deepened.

Collectively we stood as one.

As the convoy drove at speed along deserted roads, I saw a sign for Homs which I knew was not under the control of the government so I knew we were close to the violence. We stopped briefly at the roundabout on the road to Latakia. The local band came out to greet us and we were given hot chicken, bread and water to consume on the road, the exact same thing that had happened on our arrival in 2010. I desperately searched the faces of the assembled crowd hoping to recognise someone but with time being precious our escort didn't want us to be stopped for too long so we headed for a car park on the beach front of Tartous. Bearing in mind the country was at war, Tartous turned out to be a beautiful idyllic coastal town. We parked up our vans and walked along the shore before walking to our hotel.

The hotel, situated near the promenade was a welcome sight as the previous night we had slept in our vans near the border crossing so we could cross early and reach Tartous before nightfall. At the hotel we checked in, showered and I had a beer. I decided to see if I could find a shop to get some chocolate or crisps and a bottle of water. As I left the hotel I noticed some large wooden barricades with barbed wire had blocked some of the roads leading to the hotel. I was stopped on leaving the hotel and asked where I was going, to which I replied "the shop adjacent." They watched me cross the street then return. It was like a scene from a war movie. I realised our hosts were determined to protect us and I shook hands with guards manning the barricades. They were, after all, putting their lives in danger to protect us.

The next day we were up early, our destination Damascus the capital of Syria. On my first visit to Syria we never entered Damascus. Part of me was looking forward to it. Again we headed off with our military escort embedded in the convoy. As we neared the capital and joined a major motorway network joining Damascus to the rest of Syria we encountered what I assumed was the rush hour for traffic. Even our escort was unable to force our way through. We sat in the congestion moving forward slowly bumper to bumper at 10mph. I am not sure how long the delay was but it felt like hours.

Suddenly we were through the stoppage. I thought perhaps there had been an accident but shortly thereafter we arrived in downtown Damascus. We pulled up outside the hotel, parked up our vehicles and checked in at reception. I took a seat in the main foyer, beautifully cool while one or two of the organisers collected all the keys and allocated the rooms. I was given the Penthouse. I thought there must be some kind of mistake but unbeknown to me my old friend Nabil whom I'd met on the convoy and in Beirut had insisted I be given the best room in the hotel. A magnificent gesture but I must say wasted on me. I'd sleep anywhere to save a few pounds but it was a great kindness from Nabil who has strong family ties to Ireland and a young Irish daughter - a valued friend and comrade whom I rarely see but have great respect for.

We were being hosted and greeted by the Palestinian Legislative Council in Damascus and I suppose it makes sense for us to be met by the Palestinian diaspora as we were heading for Gaza. There were some media present in the hotel and camera crews who interviewed a few of the convoy members and then we were off to meet the PLC in Damascus.

It was during my chat with Nabil we were informed our delay in arriving in Damascus was not due to traffic congestion but two roadside bombs possibly car bombs that had wreaked havoc on the road we had travelled approximately one hour before. With many dead and many more injured, locals were being asked to give blood at the various hospitals. A quick decision was made that some of us on the convoy would volunteer to donate blood as an act of solidarity with the injured and with the wider Syrian society. It transpired that those who volunteered to go were all on the previous convoy. I think everyone wanted to go but in the end

Carole, Jemima, her companion, Waheed and Ash from London and I all made our way to the hospital.

A local TV crew on hearing our plans tagged along. The director was American and the crew Syrian. We were interviewed about why we gave blood. I said we were on a humanitarian aid trip to Palestine and we could not just stand idly by when people needed help. I condemned those who carried out attacks against defenceless civilians and asked them to stop. About two years later at a pro-Palestinian protest outside Belfast City Hall a young man came up to me and introduced me to his father, a Palestinian blinded by Israeli troops and forced to flee to Syria when he was a young man. The family had somehow managed to relocate to Belfast and this Belfast speaking son of a Palestinian born in Syria had been visiting family on the day of the explosion and had seen the coverage on the TV in a café. He told me he was shouting at the TV screen "I know that guy, he's from Belfast." It really is a small world.

After the meeting we all headed back to the hotel. The view from the street outside was stunning. Damascus, like Belfast, appears to be built in a basin and surrounded or encapsulated by mountains. Looking up the street onto the hills with houses dotted along its slopes reminded me of a Christmas card. I will never forget the beauty of Lebanon, Egypt, Palestine, Syria and probably the whole region is the same. Remember, they say Babylon in Iraq was the epicentre of civilisation and man came from Africa to colonise the world. Watching that breath taking vista I can only concur.

Back at the hotel for food, a chance to freshen up and a wee adventure around the surrounding streets, this time there were no road blocks just friendly day to day life in the capital. I visited a few shops and compared prices for cameras and mobile phones just to see if they were cheaper or dearer than back home. Richard and I met a lovely Syrian family, a father, mother and three kids. Richard did some magic tricks that the kids loved. Damascus like Beirut is friendly, accommodating and breath taking. I hope to return.

Next morning we left about noon with a farewell from Nabil who said he'd join us as the trip progressed and we were heading for the Syrian Jordanian border. Another delay at another border crossing, we didn't have an escort from Damascus or if we did it was much smaller. The closer we got to Jordan the further away we were from the instability and the violence. More visas, more delays which I was beginning to get used to and we were through. Country number eleven I think...

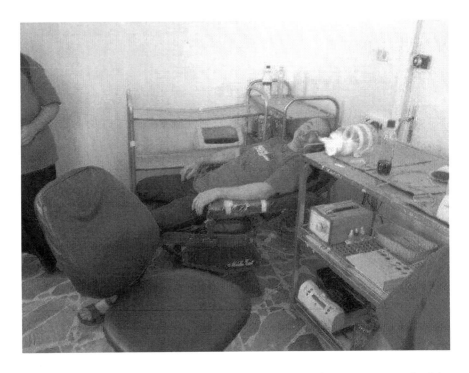

Donating blood in downtown Damascus after two road side bombs killed over 200 civilians.

Jordan

Chapter 16

Amman Jordan with the mothers of Palestinian hunger strikers.

With a police escort in Jordan we headed for Amman the capital. Another long day travelling and we arrived late at night and bang into driving through the city in the dark. Trying to juggle the need to follow the vehicle in front without colliding with the local traffic while weaving through the different lanes was challenging to say the least.

For the first time on our journey we were directed to a police parking compound and we were put on buses and taken to our accommodation. I suddenly no longer felt in control and perhaps for the first time under the control of the state. An overnight in Amman was followed the next day by a visit to a Palestinian cultural centre where we were greeted by some Palestinian youths undergoing a solidarity hunger strike coinciding with Palestinian prisoners on hunger strike in Israeli jails. They told us the stories and issues affecting the prisoners, many sentenced but never charged, how up to 800,000 or perhaps as many as 1 million men, women and children had been imprisoned since 1967 under Israel's illegal occupation of the West Bank. Can you imagine an illegal occupation jailing illegally a million people? What kind of a world do we tolerate?

Many, if not all, of the prisons are inside Historic Palestine now Israel meaning arduous and expensive travelling for the families who, upon arrival at the jails are sometimes told their loved one had been moved that morning or the previous day - a form of punishment for both family and prisoner.

I was asked if I would speak at a meeting they were having that night but our travel plans dictated otherwise. I spoke to several of the students there and explained my knowledge of the republican hunger strike of 1981. I explained the criminalisation attempts by the British government to brand Irish republican political prisoners as gunmen, gangsters and terrorists, when these men and women were clearly engaged in a national war of liberation against an imperialist coloniser - the ongoing struggle for Irish independence which now included the need for Irish reunification and an end to partition.

Before we left Amman, thousands of bottles of Penicillin were donated to the convoy so my vehicle which had carried clothes toys and food now carried lifesaving medicine. Off again directly from the car park to Aqaba on the Jordanian –West Bank border where we hoped to board a ferry going to Egypt and onwards by land to Gaza. I would say our journey so far had been pretty quick, Britain, France, Belgium, Luxembourg, Austria, Germany, Romania,

Hungary, Turkey, Syria and now Jordan. The days were sometimes long but the weeks flew in. I would say we had now been on the road 19 or 20 days to include 1 or 2 rest days. Those still left on the convoy were solid and we were nearly at our journeys end.

I had lost a bit of weight, I suppose a combination of the travelling, the heat, a lack of appetite, combined with cutting down my calorie intake had helped to reduce my waistline but I was not fading away. I did notice it on my face when I looked in the mirror. A road trip to Gaza is not a form of diet or weight control but it had that effect.

So our first day in Aqaba was very similar to our arrival in Amman, our vehicles were directed to a car park chosen by the police who then stood guard over our vehicles as we headed by bus to our hotels. It was only the next day when I needed to return to my vehicle to get my phone charger that I realised the police were babysitting the vans. I thought "that's great, no-one will damage the vehicles" but then I realised the police might be there to prevent the convoy or individuals forming the convoy from leaving unilaterally without their permission.

I remembered a conversation in Amman with the students. We were in the capital around May 14th, the anniversary of the Naqba, the term used by Palestinians to describe the Catastrophe when they were forced to flee for their lives in 1948 in the face of Zionist death squads. There was no commemoration of this pivotal day in modern Palestinian history. I had hoped to attend a rally and show support. That's when I discovered over 70% of the people of Jordan is of Palestinian descent yet it is illegal to observe, mark or officially make reference to the Naqba, it is like it never happened, such a seminal event with such devastating, eternal consequences was being ignored.

This was obviously a police state run by a feudal type monarchy. If they marched on Naqba Day it would fuel the soul and impassion the heart. The Jordanian administration didn't want that. Shameful is what it was. It reminded me of a quote by an Israeli leader referring to the Naqba, "The old will die, the young will forget." Thankfully the young will never forget. At the end of this book I will print some quotes from Israeli leaders, all their own words. You can be their judge.

Aqaba, much like Latakia previously, was to become our new home. Each morning we had breakfast and a convoy meeting. We were told the organisers were in discussion with the Egyptian authorities and any day now we hope to embark upon our sea voyage.

Now I wasn't party to these negotiations but over the following days we were told we were going then there would be a delay; next, the vehicles allowed in would only be ambulances or adapted transport so someone produced handicapped decals for all the vans; then the route was in dispute as the authorities claimed the Sinai desert was too dangerous for us to be escorted through so we offered to travel without an escort but this was not accepted.

The first hotel apartment block we took residence in no longer had any room for us due to prior bookings so we decamped to another apartment block. I was in a two roomed five bedded apartment with Richard, two of the brothers from London and the one person still on the convoy who I didn't like and had caused numerous troubles along the way. Richard had his daily routine I think as part of his disciplined military upbringing - breakfast then walk to the beach, swim, lunch, read his book and back to the hotel. I joined his daily sojourn and it suited me to enjoy his company and have a routine otherwise I'd have sat about the apartment or aimlessly strolled the streets. Evenings were taken up with finding a restaurant with internet and having a light meal with a few beers then making light conversation. A few times I headed out with Richard, sometimes with Jemima and her companion, a few times with the man from Dudley Yousef, and his companion Waheed.

Everyone had their mates, strong friendships, people they felt most comfortable with. Nabil, Kevin and Amer were leading the negotiations at this time and one day we all went to a restaurant where the food was freely given by the owner, a young successful business woman of Palestinian descent. I called round a few times after that, on one level to give back something in response to her generosity and because they served Shisha, the wacky backy as it sometimes referred. I don't know if you can get it with Hashish but what I got was flavoured tobacco, apple, Lemon, Orange, Grape or a combination of sorts.

As the days progressed into weeks my thoughts turned again to home. The delay does make people restless. We had journeyed to reach Gaza not to an enforced stopover in Aqaba. Money would also become a concern. We had accommodation which was very cheap as was food to cover each day and we still had the travel to Gaza. Viva Palestina Arabia paid for the petrol for the van throughout the journey, tolls etc. I paid for all my expenses out of my own pocket. Now I'm not complaining, this could be viewed as a subsidised trip to Gaza on the convoy but things were adding up. After about ten days people began to ask how long we could wait without a definitive decision or time frame for our arrival in Egypt.
It appeared everyone was not in agreement for our departure, three different parts of the Egyptian security apparatus had to all agree to our arrival - the military who would be guarding us, the intelligence department and an the Interior Ministry. It may have been deliberately contrived confusion or just a failure of those involved to resolve any outstanding issues.

Then one evening we were told "it's a go." We went down to the vehicles, adrenaline pumping, finally on the road again. The sailing was at midnight. I could see the ferry from where we were parked. It sailed twice weekly from Jordan to Egypt. We sat with engines running, side lights on, all our clothes and belongings on board, waiting for the lead vehicle to drive off in formation. The time was ticking by, I was beginning to think "hold on a minute, if we don't leave within the next 15 minutes it's going to go without us." We had already been waiting two hours, many had turned their engines off and were standing chatting in the car park. Then the word came it was off for that night, "grab your gear, back to the hotel everybody."

It was heart wrenching to watch the smoke rise from the boat as it sailed off oblivious of our desire to have been on board and careless of our feelings. I have to say it was the lowest point of the trip. Next morning another convoy meeting where we were told the Egyptians had reneged on their agreement at the last moment. I suspected we might have been used as a negotiating pawn. Get to the vehicles, say we are boarding and try to bluff our way to Egypt but whatever the truth the reality was we were still in Aqaba.

Again people began to question how long we could hold out. It appeared to be a waiting game and I felt the Egyptians simply had to wait us out.

The person who had been the centre of friction on the convoy decided to leave. I was disappointed for her that she wouldn't get to Gaza but glad also to see her go. Her presence had caused a distancing between me and Richard and between me and the London guy whose vehicle she had joined. It turned out he was just doing his duty as he saw it to be respectful and helpful towards an older person. Perhaps I'd misjudged him. Anyway, they were gone and I was happy for that. It transpired that she made her way to Al Arish in Egypt and approached a guy who had befriended me when I was trying to enter Gaza on a solo run.

I had told her and another convoy member of my previous escapade, who I had met, all the details. I had told one guy how to get there if that's what he wanted to do. The first guy had left us at the Turkish Syrian border, went back to Istanbul then Cairo headed down to El Arish, walked into the store my friend owned,

170

mentioned my name and asked assistance into Gaza where he was guided through the tunnels.

When our friend left us in Aqaba they too went to Cairo then to El Arish and approached my friend in the shop. He contacted me on social media and asked my thoughts on her. I was honest and said she'd caused a few problems on the convoy but she wanted to get to Gaza, however, I wasn't vouching for her as she was no friend of mine. He replied saying the request to visit Gaza had been turned down as having someone in their seventies and not very mobile was not a good idea while it was still facing possible Israeli attack. I'm disappointed they didn't get in. I put their attitude down to their personality, possibly their age, but in reality a loss to whoever they were visiting but nothing to me.

And so the end game was in sight. About two weeks in we got another call to readiness, to be prepared for another midnight run on the ferry. Bags packed, down to the vans, all systems go: adrenaline pumping, hope and excitement in equal measure. Then finally after another long wait we were again instructed to stand down. Cancelled again! The roller coaster of emotions we ran through had to be felt to be believed. I have never held the organisers responsible. There's never a guarantee you will get into Egypt and into Gaza. The craziest part of all this was we got into Egypt under Mubarak, an unelected military dictatorship, yet with a pro-Hamas, democratically elected leader in Morsi, we were getting the run around. I was thinking of all the political nuances of allowing us in, ripples in the diplomatic sea. If we get in does this mean Egypt supports Hamas? Is this snubbing Israel or America? If we do not get in does this means it's snubbing Hamas, appeasing the West and supporting Israel?

You could go round the houses trying to figure it out and round the bend too if you dwelt on it too long.

171

The bottom line was the day after the second attempt to board the ferry was cancelled they called a convoy meeting with our opinions being sought. Should we stay and wait it out or should we call this trip off? Everyone who wanted to speak was given that opportunity by Amer, Nabil and Kevin. My contribution was to say that I had about another week in me to stay but not much after that unless we were given a solid commitment and date of entry.

I also said I held no grievance with the organisers. I had joined their convoy to follow their leadership to Gaza. I felt that if we gave up the real winners would be Israel and in order for them not to win we must plan another convoy. It wasn't the getting in that really mattered but the attempt to break the siege and we must continue to do that. In conclusion I said if that was the case then to put my name first on the list for the next convoy.

There was universal disappointment when it was agreed to call off the convoy, a general feeling of Egyptian obstinacy was at the heart of us not getting in. I felt that even if we had stayed another week it would have made no difference.

One more day in Aqaba looking across the sea to the West Bank thinking and wondering if I could see Jericho from where we were now, remembering where both Pauline and I gazed across the water previously at Jordan, two separate viewing points but with one unifying question.

During our stay we had a witnessed a lovely wedding, heard the call to prayer, watched the sunset and sunrise over a beautiful sea. We had seen the West Bank and visited the Israeli checkpoint at the border. Some of the guys had visited some tourist destinations in Jordan. We had all enjoyed the sea, the beach, the food, the craic and the company. It would have been great if it had been a holiday but for all those days we had simply been on hold, waiting for Gaza.

That last day was very poignant. We all gathered at the restaurant, a wedding party and guests drove by celebrating with car horns, dances and music. I contrasted life in Belfast, that of a once peaceful Syria now being torn apart by Western intrigue, life in occupied Palestine to a peaceful prosperous Aqaba in Jordan. Palestine's illegal Zionist occupation, Syria being destroyed for a greater Israel project, Jordan, peaceful but very much a police state, compliant to the Western foreign policy that created it and non-threatening to Israel, three neighbouring countries, each facing different pressures and threats.

I wish Syria was at peace, Palestine free and Jordan gave full citizens' rights to its Palestinian population.

Down to the car park for the last time, sadness at not reaching Gaza counter balanced by an end to the seemingly endless waiting. The decision made it was time to return to Amman, then home. We arrived back in Amman, another amazing Middle Eastern capital growing out seamlessly from the sands of the desert. We had clothes, medicines, toys and food bound for Gaza. We returned to the community association we had first visited on our arrival in Amman. We gave them the keys to our vehicles and all the supplies. If we could not help the Palestinians in Gaza then we could help the diaspora here in Jordan. With farewells, hugs and kisses we left from that car park, the same car park we had left to go to Aqaba, to now travel the short distance to the airport.

On the final day in Aqaba we had booked our flights online for the journey home. I booked Amman-Paris -Dublin. We parted as friends at Amman, boarded our different flights and began the final journey home.

I wanted to go to Dublin rather that straight home to Belfast. So much had happened I needed to process it. I didn't want to get off the plane and be submerged in the guest house 24/7 so I booked a hotel room in Dublin and asked Pauline to get cover for the BnB and to meet me there.

After a long delay of several hours in Paris airport between flights, wearing my Palestinian scarf, I boarded the plane to the Irish Capital. I took the bus to central Dublin and then onto our hotel. It was great seeing Pauline and as a final entry in my video diary I interviewed Pauline asking her why she supported me in what I was doing and what her fears had been for me and the convoy on the trip. After a few days in Dublin it was back home to Belfast and a life of activism.

Bradford to Gaza. Viva Palestina Arabia convoy members.

Final night in Aqaba Jordan. With our host together with Carole and Jemimah.

Conclusion

As I sit here in Ardoyne, North Belfast, writing these memoirs I am preparing to produce a play. *My Name is Rachel Corrie* was on the stage for one night only at last year's West Belfast Festival and I hope to stage it again on behalf of Palestine Aid.

The solidarity work continues.

Appendix 1

You can be their judge. Their views publicly spoken in their own words:

"There is a huge gap between us (Jews) and our enemies, not just in ability but in morality, culture, sanctity of life, and conscience. They are our neighbours here, but it seems as if at a distance of a few hundred metres away, there are people who do not belong to our continent, to our world, but actually belong to a different galaxy."
Israeli president Moshe Katsav. (The Jerusalem Post, May 10th 2001)

"The Palestinians are like crocodiles, the more you give them meat, they want more"
Ehud Barak, Prime Minister of Israel at the time - August 28th 2000
The Jerusalem Post, August 30th 2000

"[The Palestinians are] beasts walking on two legs."
Menahim Begin, speech to the Knesset, quoted in Amnon Kapeliouk, "*Begin and the Beasts*". New Statesman, 25 June 1982.

"The Palestinians would be crushed like grasshoppers ... heads smashed against the boulders and walls."
Israeli Prime Minister (at the time) in a speech to Jewish settlers
New York Times April 1st 1988

"When we have settled the land, all the Arabs will be able to do about it will be to scurry around like drugged cockroaches in a bottle."
Raphael Eitan, Chief of Staff of the Israeli Defence Forces, New York Times, 14th April 1983.

"How can we return the occupied territories? There is nobody to return them to."
Golda Maier, March 8th 1969.

"There was no such thing as Palestinians, they never existed."
Golda Maier, Israeli Prime Minister June 15th 1969

"The thesis that the danger of genocide was hanging over us in June 1967 and that Israel was fighting for its physical existence is only bluff, which was born and developed after the war."
Israeli General Matityahu Peled, Ha'aretz, 19th March 1972.

"If I were an Arab leader, I would never sign an agreement with Israel. It is normal; we have taken their country. It is true God promised it to us, but how could that interest them? Our God is not theirs. There has been Anti - Semitism, the Nazis, Hitler, Auschwitz, but was that their fault ? They see but one thing: we have come and we have stolen their country. Why would they accept that?"
David Ben Gurion (the first Israeli Prime Minister): Quoted by Nahum Goldmann in Le Paraddoxe Juif (The Jewish Paradox), pp121.

"We must do everything to ensure they (the Palestinians) never do return. The old will die and the young will forget."
Ben Gurion,1948 : Assuring his fellow Zionists that Palestinians will never come back to their homes.

"We have to kill all the Palestinians unless they are resigned to live here as slaves."
Chairman Heilbrun of the Committee for the Re-election of General Shlomo Lahat, the mayor of Tel Aviv, October 1983.

"Every time we do something you tell me America will do this and will do that . . . I want to tell you something very clear: Don't worry about American pressure on Israel. We, the Jewish people, control America, and the Americans know it."
Israeli Prime Minister, Ariel Sharon, October 3rd 2001, to Shimon Peres, as reported on Kol Yisrael radio. (Certainly the FBI's cover-up of the Israeli spy ring/phone tap scandal suggests that Mr. Sharon may not have been joking.)

"We declare openly that the Arabs have no right to settle on even one centimeter of Eretz Israel... Force is all they do or ever will understand. We shall use the ultimate force until the Palestinians come crawling to us on all fours."
Rafael Eitan, Chief of Staff of the Israeli Defense Forces - Gad Becker, Yediot Ahronot 13th April 1983, New York Times 14th April 1983.

" ... we should prepare to go over to the offensive with the aim of smashing Lebanon, Trans-Jordan and Syria... The weak point in the Arab coalition is Lebanon [for] the Moslem regime is artificial

and easy to undermine. A Christian state should be established...
When we smash the [Arab] Legions strength and bomb Amman,
we will eliminate Transjordan, too, and then Syria will fall. If
Egypt still dares to fight on, we shall bomb Port Said, Alexandria,
and Cairo." David Ben-Gurion, May 1948, to the General Staff.
From Ben-Gurion, A Biography, by Michael Ben-Zohar, Delacorte,
New York 1978.

"We must use terror, assassination, intimidation, land
confiscation, and the cutting of all social services to rid the Galilee
of its Arab population."
Israel Koenig, "The Koenig Memorandum"

"Jewish villages were built in the place of Arab villages. You do
not even know the names of these Arab villages, and I do not
blame you because geography books no longer exist. Not only do
the books not exist, the Arab villages are not there either. Nahlal
arose in the place of Mahlul; Kibbutz Gvat in the place of Jibta;
Kibbutz Sarid in the place of Huneifis; and Kefar Yehushua in the
place of Tal al-Shuman. There is not a single place built in this
country that did not have a former Arab population."
Moshe Dayan, address to the Technion, Haifa, reported in Haaretz,
April 4th 1969.

"We walked outside, Ben-Gurion accompanying us. Allon
repeated his question, What is to be done with the Palestinian
population?' Ben-Gurion waved his hand in a gesture which said
'Drive them out!'"
Yitzhak Rabin, leaked censored version of Rabin memoirs,
published in the New York Times, 23rd Oct

"We shall reduce the Arab population to a community of woodcutters and waiters"
Rabin's description of the conquest of Lydda, after the completion of Plan Dalet Uri Lubrani, PM Ben-Gurion's special adviser on Arab Affairs, 1960. From "The Arabs in Israel" by Sabri Jiryas.

"There are some who believe that the non-Jewish population, even in a high percentage, within our borders will be more effectively under our surveillance; and there are some who believe the contrary, i.e., that it is easier to carry out surveillance over the activities of a neighbor than over those of a tenant. [I] tend to support the latter view and have an additional argument:...the need to sustain the character of the state which will henceforth be Jewish...with a non-Jewish minority limited to 15 percent. I had already reached this fundamental position as early as 1940 [and] it is entered in my diary."
Joseph Weitz, head of the Jewish Agency's Colonization Department. From Israel: an Apartheid State by Uri Davis, p.5

"Everybody has to move, run and grab as many hilltops as they can to enlarge the settlements because everything we take now will stay ours... Everything we don't grab will go to them."
Ariel Sharon, Israeli Foreign Minister, addressing a meeting of militants from the extreme right-wing Tsomet Party, Agence France Presse, November 15th 1998.

"It is the duty of Israeli leaders to explain to public opinion, clearly and courageously, a certain number of facts that are forgotten with time. The first of these is that there is no Zionism,colonialization or Jewish State without the eviction of the Arabs and the expropriation of their lands."
Yoram Bar Porath, Yediot Aahronot, of 14th July 1972.

"Spirit the penniless population across the frontier by denying it employment... Both the process of expropriation and the removal of the poor must be carried out discreetly and circumspectly."
Theodore Herzl, founder of the World Zionist Organization, speaking of the Arabs of Palestine, Complete Diaries, June 12th 1895 entry.

"One million Arabs are not worth a Jewish fingernail."
Rabbi Yaacov Perrin, Feb. 27th 1994 [Source: N.Y. Times, Feb. 28, 1994, p. 1]

"We Jews, we are the destroyers and will remain the destroyers. Nothing you can do will meet our demands and needs. We will forever destroy because we want a world of our own."
(You Gentiles, by Jewish Author Maurice Samuels, p. 155).

"We will have a world government whether you like it or not. The only question is whether that government will be achieved by conquest or consent."
(Jewish Banker Paul Warburg, February 17, 1950, as he testified before the U.S. Senate).

"We will establish ourselves in Palestine whether you like it or not...You can hasten our arrival or you can equally retard it. It is however better for you to help us so as to avoid our constructive powers being turned into a destructive power which will overthrow the world."
(Chaim Weizmann, Published in "Judische Rundschau," No. 4, 1920)

"Our race is the Master Race. We are divine gods on this planet.

We are as different from the inferior races as they are from insects. In fact, compared to our race, other races are beasts and animals, cattle at best. Other races are considered as human excrement. Our destiny is to rule over the inferior races. Our earthly kingdom will be ruled by our leader with a rod of iron. The masses will lick our feet and serve us as our slaves."
Israeli prime Minister Menachem Begin in a speech to the Knesset [Israeli Parliament] quoted by Amnon Kapeliouk, "*Begin and the Beasts*," New Statesman, June 25, 1982

"Tell me, do the evil men of this world have a bad time? They hunt and catch whatever they feel like eating. They don't suffer from indigestion and are not punished by Heaven. I want Israel to join that club. Maybe the world will then at last begin to fear us instead of feeling sorry. Maybe they will start to tremble, to fear our madness instead of admiring our nobility. Let them tremble; let them call us a mad state. Let them understand that we are a savage country, dangerous to our surroundings, not normal, that we might go wild, that we might start World War Three just like that, or that we might one day go crazy and burn all the oil fields in the Middle East. Even if you'll prove to me that the present war is a dirty immoral war, I don't care. We shall start another war, kill and destroy more and more. And do you know why it is all worth it? Because it seems that this war has made us more unpopular among the civilized world. We'll hear no more of that nonsense about the unique Jewish morality. No more talk about a unique people being a light upon the nations. No more uniqueness and no more sweetness and light. Good riddance."
Former Israeli Prime Minister Ariel Sharon

Read more: www.whatreallyhappened.com
http://www.whatreallyhappened.com/WRHARTICLES/palestinians.php#ixzz4kY8brDfP

183

Appendix 2

Timeline of Palestine's History

1799 – 1946

1799 – Napoleon offers Palestine as a homeland to Jews

1882 – Rishon Le Zion, a major Zionist settlement is established in Palestine

1885 – The term 'Zionism' is first coined

1896 – Theodor Herzl publishes *Der Judenstaat,* calling for the creation of a Jewish state

1897 – The first Zionist Congress is held in Switzerland, the first Zionist organisation is founded

1907 – Zionist leader Chaim Weizmann visits Palestine for the first time

1908 – Palestinian writer Najib Nassar publishes *Al-Karmel* newspaper opposing Zionist colonisation

1915 – Zionist British cabinet member Herbert Samuel writes *The Future of Palestine*, a secret memorandum calling on his cabinet colleagues to support Zionist settlement in Palestine

1916 – Sykes-Picot secret agreement is signed dividing the Middle East between the French and British

1917 – Balfour Declaration created. Britain promises 'A Jewish National Home' on Arab land

1919 – Washington's King Crane Commission is conducted on the future of Palestine

1922 – The League of Nations approves the British mandate for Palestine and its purpose of helping establish a Jewish homeland

1929 – Al-Buraq uprising takes place, the first mass protests against increased Jewish immigration to Palestine

1933 – Mass protests against Jewish immigration to Palestine

1935 – Izz Ad-Din Al-Qassam, a revolutionary leader in Palestine is killed by British forces

1936 – Six-month long general strike takes place in Palestine to protest Jewish immigration

1937 – Peel Commission recommends the partition of Palestine and transfer of Palestinians from land allocated to a Jewish state

1938 – Armed Zionist group, Irgin, launches a series of attacks against Palestinians

1939 – Britain smashes the three year long Arab revolt

1942 – Zionist conference is held at the Biltmore Hotel in New York City solidifying US-Zionist relations

1946 – Irgin bombs the King David Hotel in Jerusalem killing 91 people

1947 – 1949

Over 80% of Palestinians in what became Israel were expelled and approximately 80% of Palestinian land was seized by Zionists.

1947 – UN adopts Resolution 181, a partition plan for Palestine, Palestinians reject it

1948 January – Armed Zionist group, Haganah bombs the Semiramis Hotel in Jerusalem. More than 20 people are killed

February – Zionist forces attack the village of Qisarya near Haifa, an early example of ethnic cleansing

April – Stern gang and Irgin forces massacre Palestinians in the village of Dayr Yassin, near Jerusalem

May – The state of Israel is created sparking regional conflict. The US and Soviet Union recognise Israel immediately

August – Stern gang assassinates Folke Bernadotte, a Swedish diplomat and the UN-appointed mediator in Palestine
December – UN Assembly passes Resolution 194, affirming the right of return of Palestinian refugees

1949 – Feb-July Armistice Agreements are signed between Israel and its neighbouring Arab countries: Lebanon, Syria, Jordan and Egypt

December – UN establishes UNRWA, an agency for Palestinian Refugees

1950 – 1967

After the tumultuous events of 1948, 150,000 Palestinians remained in Israel and were eventually granted citizenship. However, they were subjected to military rule until 1966. After the conquest of the West Bank and Gaza Strip in 1967, Israel began its military control over Palestinians living in the Occupied Palestinian Territory.

1950 – Jordan assumes administrative control of the West Bank

1956 – Israel massacres Palestinians in the villages of Qalqilys, Kufr Qassem and Khan Younis

1964 – The Palestinian Liberation Organisation is formed in Cairo

1966 – Israel massacres Palestinians in the village of As-Samu'

1967 – Israel occupies the rest of historic Palestine including the Gaza Strip and the West Bank, as well as the Syrian Golan Heights and the Egyptian Sinai.

1967 – The UN Security Council passes Resolution 242 calling on Israel to withdraw from territories it occupied in 1967

1968 – 1992

Following Israel's occupation of the rest of historic Palestine, it began building settlements in the West Bank and Gaza Strip. In these colonies, Jewish settlers are allowed to carry weapons under the protection of the Israeli army. In 1987, after 20 years of brutal military occupation, the First Intifada began in the Occupied Palestinian Territory.

1970 – Israel attacks Palestinian fighters during 'Black September' in Jordan

1973 – The UN Security Council passes Resolution 338 following the October War, calling for a ceasefire and, once again, for Israel to withdraw from territories it occupied in 1967

1974 – The Arab League recognises the PLO as the sole, legitimate representative body of the Palestinian people

1976 – Israel confiscates thousands of hectares from Palestinian citizens. Mass protests organised in response were brutally put down: now 'Land Day' is commemorated every year.

1978 – Egypt and Israel sign the Camp David Accords

1982 – Israel invades Lebanon

1982 – UN International day of solidarity with the Palestinian people

1987 – The first intifada is launched in the occupied Palestinian Territory

1988 – The PLO accepts UN Resolutions 242 and 338, recognising the state of Israel

1991 – The Madrid Peace Conference ends without a breakthrough

1992 – More multilateral talks take place but the Palestinians are no closer to statehood

1993 – 2014

The secret negotiations between the PLO and Israel that concluded in 1993 heralded a new chapter of modern Palestinian history. For some, the Oslo Accords raised hopes for peace. For others, it dashed them entirely.

1993 – The PLO and Israel sign the Declaration of Principles on Interim Self-Government Arrangements (Oslo I)

1995 – The PLO and Israel sign an interim Agreement granting the Palestinians some autonomy in certain parts of the West Bank and Gaza Strip (Oslo II)

1997 – The PLO and Israel sign an Agreement that requires Israeli forces to partially withdraw from Hebron

2000 – The PLO and Israel renew final status negotiations at the Camp David II summit

2002 – Israel reoccupies Palestinian cities in the West Bank in the wake of the second intifada

2004 – Yasser Arafat dies

2005 – Israel conducts its 'disengagement' from Gaza

2006 – War breaks out between Israel and Hezbollah in Lebanon

2008 – Peace activists on two boats drop anchor in Gaza, breaking the Israeli blockade

2012 – Israel attacks Gaza once more, in what it calls 'Operation Pillar of Defense'

2014 – Israel launches the biggest assault on Gaza since 1967, 'Operation Protective Edge'

2015 - Israeli Prime Minister Netanyahu Says No to Two-State Solution on Eve of Election while the Vatican recognises State of Palestine in New Treaty

2017 - Israel Passes Law Retroactively Legalizing Almost 4,000 Settler Homes Built on Palestinian Land

Feb. 15, 2017 - US President Trump Open to One-State Solution, Change in Decades-Long US Policy of Advocating Two-State Solution

Apr. 6, 2017 - Russia Recognizes West Jerusalem as Future Capital of Israel and East Jerusalem as Capital of Future Palestinian State

May 1, 2017 - Hamas Declares Willingness to Accept Interim Palestinian State alongside Israel (pre-1967 Boundaries)

My sincere thanks to Al Jazeera and the Palestine Remix Interactive Platform of Al Jazeera Network for allowing me to reproduce this timeline here.

189

Printed in Great Britain
by Amazon

16798045R00119